AUTHORITY AND INEQUALITY UNDER CAPITALISM AND SOCIALISM

Authority and Inequality under Capitalism and Socialism

BARRINGTON MOORE JR

CLARENDON PRESS · OXFORD

1987

Oxford University Press, Walton Street, Oxford OX2 6DP
Oxford New York Toronto
Delhi Bombay Calcutta Madras Karachi
Petaling Jaya Singapore Hong Kong Tokyo
Nairobi Dar es Salaam Cape Town
Melbourne Auckland
and associated companies in
Beirut Berlin Ibadan Nicosia

Oxford is a trade mark of Oxford University Press

Published in the United States
by Oxford University Press, New York

British Library Cataloguing in Publication Data

Moore, Barrington
Authority and inequality under capitalism and socialism.
— (The Tanner lectures on human values; 1985)
1. Socialism   2. Capitalism
I. Title   II. Series
335   HX73
ISBN 0–19–828540–X

Library of Congress Cataloging in Publication Data
data available

Set by Katerprint Typesetting Services, Oxford
Printed in Great Britain by
Billing & Sons Ltd
Worcester

TO E.C.M.

PREFACE AND ACKNOWLEDGEMENTS

THIS book is an expanded and considerably revised version of the Tanner Lectures on Human Values that I had the honour and pleasure of delivering at Oxford University, in May of 1985. The Tanner lectureship was a munificent one that took care of both necessities and amenities. For this generosity both Mrs Moore and I are grateful. We are especially grateful for the unobtrusive yet warmly supportive hospitality of the Master of Brasenose College, Barry Nicholas and his wife Hildegart. They guided us wisely in the ways of Oxford, thereby enabling us to glimpse from the inside the workings and customs of that ancient, proud, and distinguished institution. Among those who attended the lectures and talked with me afterwards or took part in a lively discussion at the end of the series there were several whose comments have had an impact on the revisions made for this version.

A pleasant discussion with Andrew Schuller of the Oxford University Press, together with the subsequent critical observations by the Press's readers, have led me to add several pages of new text and make other emendations. Thus this text is about twice as long as the material presented orally. For the purpose of the oral presentation I could give only about half of each lecture following a very sketchy account of the themes that had to be omitted due to the pressure of time.

A large portion of the debts incurred in the preparation of these lectures falls on the North American side of the Atlantic. As in the case of all my professional work for many years, Harvard University provided indispensable support and encouragement, including the resources of one of the world's greatest libraries. The presentation of portions of the last chapter before discussion groups from the Department of History and the Center for European Studies led to substantial modifications that I hope were improvements. At the Russian Research Center I enjoyed the company and on occasion the guidance of a number of informed and lively specialists on both Russia and China. It may also be appropriate to mention here that I did not come to the presentation of these lectures as a complete novice. At various points in my teaching career at Harvard I gave courses on the USA, the USSR, and China, which may merely mean that I have become deeply rooted in the errors of my ways. At the Russian Research Center Mary Towle has gone out of her way to provide friendly support above and beyond the basic material prerequisites for scholarly research and writing. For decades Rose Di Benedetto has typed my manuscipts which I hope are not so hard to decipher as many authors claim about their own. Over the years she has done a great many things for me beyond the call of duty and, I have noticed on occasion, for others as well. But she has defended my interests with such a special intensity—if not ferocity—that she has in effect become a member of our family as we have of hers.

In the form of support and advice my wife's help has been precious to me on both sides of the Atlantic. From the very beginning of my scholarly career she has been the first to read and criticize the texts of my books. She has always verified the references and many a time dug up valuable information for me to ponder. It is unlikely that I have encountered in my life so far anything like the adversity I deserve, but if my share does come along in the future, I know I can count on her support then too. Best of all she remains a marvellous companion on skis and under sail, as well as other activities that are part of life's real fun. Hence this book, too, is dedicated to her.

CONTENTS

I

INTRODUCTION

FOR a long time I had wanted to review the available evidence about
the social and political roles of authority and inequality under capitalism and socialism. These studies that have grown out of the Tanner
Lectures at Oxford (May 1985) ask chiefly: how and why do capitalism
and socialism work the way they have come to work? In my tentative
answers the emphasis is on bureaucracy, because from the standpoint
of such an inquiry it is the most salient trait shared by the capitalist
and socialist societies examined: the USA, the USSR, and the
People's Republic of China. It offers us a useful searchlight, I believe,
to reveal key differences and similarities in how these societies
work.

The only claim that these studies have on the reader's attention rests
upon the validity of causal interpretations and the extent to which they
may add to our understanding of very significant social practices. (I
cannot offer new facts nor keep abreast of current events. For such
data I must refer the reader to references in the notes.) To avoid
possible misunderstanding let me emphasize that an interest in everchanging social structures and cultural milieux does not preclude a
belief in the importance of human choices and actions. Painful choices
make splendid political rhetoric in liberal societies. Nevertheless the
choice, and even the pain, can be real. In socialist societies the choice
is often masked, and so is the pain, behind a cloud of rhetoric about
the inevitable march of history. Yet the element of individual choice
among several possible policies may well be more important in a
socialist dictatorship than a liberal capitalist regime.

My reasons for choosing authority and inequality as central themes
rest on the fact that in every society with a written language, as well as
numerous non-literate societies, systems of authority and inequality
have very powerful effects on every individual in that society. In
a complex society the system of authority and inequality allocates
individuals to specific slots in the social order and comes close to
determining the kind of treatment an individual can expect to receive

in that slot. The term authority implies the existence of voluntary obedience based on the belief that the commands have a morally acceptable source. (It may not be morally acceptable to everybody, as in the case of commands based on doctrines of racial or religious supremacy.) Without this moral component, authority is replaced by force and fraud. But in real life the distinction between authority and naked power is often hard to draw. Perhaps I have stretched the concept of authority beyond the breaking-point in discussing some aspects of Stalin's rule. Yet no great harm is done, if the causal analysis itself is accurate. Being a stickler for conceptual consistency can become an end in itself that prevents clear thinking about the real world. In any case conceptual clarity is possible only *after* one has learned about something.

Partly because the evidence on inequality is thin for socialist societies and partly because the social relationships of authority seem to me somewhat more interesting, the discussion concentrates on the workings and limits of authority, presenting no more than essential highlights about inequality in all three societies. In this connection it is appropriate to mention that I have no faith whatever in the prospect of a classless society, though I am quite ready to change my views if anyone presents compelling evidence during my remaining years on this earth. The main reasons for this scepticism will appear in more detail at relevant points in the text. In addition to the requirements of the division of labour there is the need for authority to co-ordinate the activities of individuals and groups to produce the social product. In modern societies this social product includes both tangible objects, such as certain sizes of nuts and bolts, and intangibles, such as rough facsimiles of internal peace and justice.

There may be some who will take this scepticism about equality as a symptom of ineradicable conservatism rather than a response to evidence and argument. For those who choose to read these pages it may be helpful if I set out very briefly my conception of social science because it has had a strong influence not only on the choice of topics for inquiry but also on the way of treating them.

This conception is not at all original. At the end of the Second World War the University of Chicago asked me to take part in teaching an introductory course in the social sciences. Somewhere in the mimeographed material explaining and justifying the course there was a remark to the effect that nearly all serious social inquiry was an attempt to ascertain the prospects for and obstacles to a free and rational society. This idea became a guide for my teaching and research.

Obviously that is not the only objective for social science. There is also that of seeking laws and regularities in human behaviour or, at a somewhat less rigorous and pretentious level of discourse, interesting patterns of thought and behaviour. As a beginning social scientist I had accepted the prevailing view that the ultimate object of social science was to discover laws of social behaviour analogous to the laws of physics and chemistry. With the passage of time I noticed that social scientists had not discovered any laws or regularities that commanded the kind of assent that occurs in the natural sciences. Suspecting that something might be wrong with the traditional project of social science, I turned with a sense of relief to the politically oriented types of inquiry suggested by the Chicago intellectual environment. These forms of inquiry demand the same degree of detachment, impartiality, accuracy, and objectivity in the analysis of evidence and argument as does any other scholarly undertaking. On the other hand, to the extent that the causal analyses (in which I am most interested) are expected to yield political and even moral appraisals, the work itself becomes more attractive, though this is not necessarily true for everybody. There are good scholars who detest anything that smacks of usefulness, politics, or morality. Those of us who feel otherwise should not turn up our noses at such scholarship. Instead we should seek what enlightenment there is to be found in it, which is often a great deal.

In due course, social scientists may find that they must combine inquiries into prospects for and obstacles to a free and rational society with the search for laws and regularities in social behaviour. Thus the assertion that equality is unlikely in any complex society has to rest upon powerful historical trends that take on the character of laws about social behaviour.

Somewhere along the line I learned to combine this inquiry into the prospects for a free and rational society with an upside-down utilitarianism that asked how much misery any given social arrangement caused, as well as who benefited from the misery. These are not the sort of questions one asks every minute. But they do influence the sort of facts one looks for.

At the same time an investigator who really wants to find out something about human societies must *not* stick to looking for a theoretically predetermined brand of facts. My advice and practice on this score flies in the face of those who believe that one has to define problems carefully in advance of research and, where possible, formulate hypotheses to be tested with carefully processed evidence. Such counsel is not all wrong, though in my judgement it *can* sterilize inquiry if taken too seriously. My main objection is that it is not enough. One needs something of the skills and outlook of the old-fashioned naturalist who treated facts gently and cautiously, trying to understand how living structures worked in their natural setting. Above all, one has to allow unexpected facts to surface, indeed encourage them to surface and force our attention to their possible meaning. Without a willingness to face surprises—indeed an eagerness to seek out surprises—there can be no such thing as intellectual progress.

Because so much has been written about freedom and rationality, the words free and rational may easily cause some puzzlement. For the purposes of social analysis the important point to remember is that these terms have a strong historical component even though there is a constant element too. The technological and intellectual possibilities for the development of freedom and rationality were not the same in ancient Athens as in modern industrial societies. 'Free' to me implies the absence of constraints in making choices that stand a good chance of reducing human misery, one's own or that of other people. 'Rational' is a bit more complicated. One common meaning limits it to the choice of the best means available in the light of current knowledge for attaining a given end, no matter what the end may be. It may be a very destructive one, such as running an extermination camp. The other usage rejects the indeterminacy of ends in order to reach the conclusion that a rational society is one that accords with reason. Though this usage makes me uneasy because it carries overtones of a well-ordered and moderately comfortable prison, dispensing with any notion of rational social ends leaves us in an even worse position. My solution, once again, is to resort to the negative and assert that social institutions which create unnecessary human suffering are indeed irrational. Whether or not the suffering is unnecessary is a factual question, though hardly an easy one to answer in specific cases.

One more point deserves emphasis. Freedom and rationality may at times come into conflict with each other. One cannot always expect to increase freedom and rationality at the same time. De Tocqueville hinted at this limitation when, in speaking of the *ancien régime*, he observed somewhat ironically that the basis of freedom is an ancient abuse. A well-endowed university, protected by longstanding custom and statute from the prying eyes of anti-intellectual legislators, can on occasion provide the security that encourages intellectual freedom and exploration. At any rate most of us would like to think so.

The opposite kind of situation, where freedom and rationality have supported one another and marched forward together, is historically more familiar. Human rational faculties during the eighteenth and nineteenth centuries helped to liberate us from the divine right of kings and other untenable justifications for authority. Likewise, rationality undermined faith in magic, superstition, and religion. The critical and corrosive power of reason has been enormous. Constructively, in the sense of designing and building social institutions the way an architect constructs a house, human rationality has few if any successes to its credit. A major cause of this widespread failure, in my opinion, is the ignorance of many ambitious social theorists about the human materials with which they must work. Like many a modern architect, they design handsome buildings in which it is impossible to live and work. To ignore relevant facts for the sake of beautiful theories is a deformation of rationality.

Finally, to avoid misunderstanding I will confess that I do not believe that a completely free and rational society will ever come to pass. The obstacles are just too great. But we probably can do much better than we have during most of the twentieth century. Looking for the forces that promote such a society, as well as the obstacles to its creation, raises historical and social inquiry from the level of parlour games toward that of objective analysis of major contemporary and perennial issues. Such concerns are far from new in the social sciences. They receded into the background, however, as social scientists sought greater respectability through precision and objectivity. Precision and objectivity are of course essential to the scholarly enterprise. To be fruitful, on the other hand, these qualities have to be directed toward worthwhile objectives.

The selection of cases for this study deserves a few comments. Subject to the constraints of limited time for a large subject I again used negative criteria. What would one think of any discussion of capitalism that omitted the USA? What would one think of an analysis of socialism that did not discuss the two main contemporary versions, the USSR and China? Other existing variants of both capitalism and socialism deserve study: Scandinavian welfare capitalism, British capitalism and continental forms, Japan, as well as satellite socialism in Eastern Europe. The main interest in such inquiries might be to set out more clearly the range of variation in capitalist and socialist societies and to discover in what ways they are more or less humane than the capitalism and socialism of the great powers. Yet there are reasons to doubt that whatever humane features exist in the smaller and generally dependent countries can have much influence on the dominant powers. In the first place, the great powers have been highly suspicious of social experiments in their sphere of influence. In the second place, the situations faced by innovating great powers subject to the constraints of international power politics is quite different from that of a small country in a back-eddy of world politics. I will return to these issues briefly toward the end of the final chapter.

The main purpose of each chapter is to set out and explain those features of authority and inequality that are the most significant in each case. For this reason I have not tried to produce for comparative purposes three complete parallel descriptions of the corresponding social arrangements in the United States, the USSR, and China. Such an account runs the risk of distorting the meaning of important social practices and institutions that are the unique products of a unique historical experience. An exposition that forces the evidence through a conceptual sieve for the sake of a 'higher' form of social theory, thereby distorting the natural patterns among social facts and obliterating unique causal chains, turns into a pretentious deception. It is not science but pseudo-science.

These critical observations do not imply a general rejection of the comparative method. In the opening pages of the last chapter I have tried to extract the theoretical yield from these three cases. Comparisons may be most enlightening when they draw attention to different ways of attaining the same end, such as in Soviet and Chinese systems of coercion and population control. These two systems can in turn be compared with the relatively non-coercive yet at times suffocating ways of obtaining consensus in the USA and other liberal democratic regimes. Perhaps the main virtue of the comparative method is to clear the mind of false laws or social imperatives. To put the point crudely, there is more than one way to skin a cat. Yet in the end the cat loses its skin anyway, which is what matters to the cat. Inescapably, the range of alternatives does narrow for both cats and human policy-makers.

At this point some readers might find it helpful in keeping their bearings later, if the author were to take them at a brisk trot through the book as a whole, pointing out some of the main sights on the way. The first chapter, on the USA, is the shortest partly because I felt that most readers knew a great deal already, much of it just from the experience of living in a liberal democracy. In going through the descriptive literature on the United States the evidence for an ambiguous and ambivalent behaviour in relation to authority and inequality became, at least for me, very convincing. Despite this ambivalence, bureaucracy has become as significant an aspect of authority in the United States as in any other economically advanced liberal society. Therefore this chapter introduces the reader to some of the ways that bureaucracy works, not only in liberal societies, but to a considerable extent in socialist (and for that matter fascist) ones as well. In regard to equality Americans evidently want no more than equality of opportunity. Even if all the contestants in life's race began the race at the same starting line, which of course never happens, the results of the race would be very unequal. Despite stiff inheritance taxes, the inequalities are passed on to the next generation. I have tried to show the historical conditions under which the hostility to authority and acceptance of inequality grew up, with some comments on its curious persistence under advanced industrialism. There is a great deal more to be learned about this persistence. At this point I can only suggest that it may to a great extent reflect the resentments of the little man who has 'made it' by climbing a few rungs up the economic ladder where he then finds all moves blocked in a world of corporate and governmental bureaucracies. It would be natural for this resentment to grasp at old traditions of individualism that justify hostility to rules and regulations which interfere with the immediate gratifications of limited success. The media also produce a keen awareness that élites in the USA do not always play by the rules. Why, then, should the rest have to obey them?

The third chapter on the Soviet. Union, like the fourth one on China, begins with a review of both the historical obstacles to a liberal and democratic resolution to the country's internal tensions prior to the revolutions, and the limited indigenous movements toward a liberal and democratic society. Following the Bolshevik revolution that put an end to these trends, Lenin found himself leading a concerted movement toward order, discipline, and productivity. Lenin and his close associates sought to stamp out forms of radicalism native to Russian peasants and industrial workers and semi-anarchist currents surviving in the Bolshevik Party itself. This reaffirmation of authority—revolutionary authority now—appeared in its most revealing form with the attempts to reimpose managerial authority in the factory, a topic discussed at some length in this chapter. Against grumbling and even outright opposition in the Party, Lenin founded the traditions of authority and inequality and instituted the use of police terror to make them stick. Stalin greatly intensified these features of 'really existing socialism' as he carried out the 'revolution from above' (Stalin's own term) in the form of forced collectivization of agriculture and high-speed industrialization. Essentially, the revolution from above was a pre-emptive coup against the restoration of capitalism as a result of forces released by the relaxation of controls under Lenin's New Economic Policy. A major consequence of the revolution from above was an enormous intensification of terror from above. The terror, however, does not seem to me to have been a necessary or unavoidable result of collectivization and industrialization. Instead, the use of terror on such a wide scale seems to have derived from Stalin's highly suspicious and vindictive character. Coming and going in waves, it lasted until Stalin's death. Especially in the decimation of officer corps in the armed forces, the terror injured rather than strengthened the regime.

Stalin's successors greatly reduced the terror, perhaps as a concession to the new technocrats and bureaucrats upon whom the top leaders depended. Except for limited tinkering, on the other hand, they have done nothing about the enormous administrative apparatus that controls the economy which, we are told, is by now inefficient and, in many areas, technically antiquated. Reforms *à la chinoise*, aimed at increasing grass-roots incentives and local initiative in order to increase production, appear to be out of bounds in the Soviet Union for now, because the top leaders fear that socialism could disintegrate without strong controls for allocating resources according to political rather than economic criteria. Even Gorbachev has so far given no indication of reforms that would change the system of incentives to improve productivity and efficiency. Instead, he has done no more than crack the administrative whip meting out exemplary punishment to a few notoriously corrupt officials and asking for a more ambitious plan. Such moves are in a classic Bolshevik style and, therefore, probably reassuring in the present Soviet context. Whether they will do any good is another matter.

The discussion of the Soviet case closes with a review of the evidence about the ladder of inequality under Soviet socialism, comparable to a similar discussion of the corresponding ladder in the United States. Though the determinants of position on the ladder are different, mainly economic in the USA and mainly political in the

USSR, the distance from the bottom rung to the top one turns out to be about the same in both cases. In other words, there is as much inequality in the Soviet Union as the United States. As will appear shortly, the same holds true for China.

In important ways Mao was very different from Stalin. At no time does Mao appear to have been the sole policy-maker in China. While Stalin broke cleanly with egalitarian ideals, Mao continued to cherish them to the end of his life. Stalin issued the famous slogan 'Cadres decide everything'. Mao, on the other hand, remained hostile to bureaucracy until the very end. Yet, despite Mao's hostility, China rapidly generated a huge bureaucracy shortly after the Communist victory in 1949.

Thus, on account of Mao's hostility to bureaucracy, the Chinese case reveals a great deal more about the social forces that generate a huge bureaucracy than does the Russian example, even though the dynamics were similar in both cases. Here it may well be correct to use the term 'social imperative'. After the triumph of a revolution Communist leaders need big bureaucracies for at least two purposes. One is to direct the economy and promote rapid growth without the stimulus and direction of the market—in fact frequently against cues coming from latent markets. In the second place, Communist leaders need a large apparatus of coercion and persuasion to elicit the desired attitudes and behaviour from the underlying population. For a time there may be talk of creating a new socialist human being, free of capitalist selfish acquisitiveness and oriented toward the welfare of the community. This sort of talk makes a bigger impression on left-leaning Western intellectuals than on ordinary people who have to come to terms with 'really existing socialism'.

It is worth pausing to observe that traditional Marxist theory did not anticipate the emergence of a socialist Leviathan out of a socialist revolution. Indeed, Marx's anticipations were almost exactly the opposite. He expected the natural evolution of capitalism to create an impoverished proletariat that would, in the course of its impoverishment, lose all attachment to capitalism and become good revolutionary tinder. In other words capitalism would create the new socialist personality *before* the revolution occurred. Just how and why this transformation would take place is not clear, at least not to me. I suspect that there is nothing more here than a dubious relic of Hegel. Any really impoverished proletariat, such as those in many a Third-World city, is liable to have a heavy criminal and asocial component that for a time presents severe problems even for a ruthless socialist system of law and order.

Lenin applied the same reasoning to the dominant classes of capitalist society. Capitalism, he argued before the Bolshevik Revolution, had in the course of its growth so simplified the functions of supervision and accounting that any literate file-clerk could perform them. In other words capitalism had rendered the managerial apparatus superfluous. The rest of the bureaucratic apparatus of the capitalist state, mainly the military forces and the police, amounted to nothing more than the repressive machinery at the disposal of the bourgeoisie. Therefore the socialist revolution when it came, could and should simply smash the existing bureaucracy.

Chinese Communists have put far more effort into mitigating the arbitrary effects of bureaucracy than have their Soviet comrades. The main device is to give bureaucrats a stint of manual labour, which Chinese Communists, at least in their official rhetoric, regard as morally purifying. Another more general notion is that of the mass line, expressed in the slogan 'from the masses to the masses'. This is a short-hand expression of the Party's alleged method of rule: to take the vague and confused demands of the masses, purify and refine these demands to the point where they can make the basis for a concrete plan of action, and then bring this plan of action back to the masses. The idea is a Communist version of *vox populi, vox dei*. In practice it is the leading Party faction of the moment that determines which masses are authentic masses and which policies will meet the requirements and demands of the authentic masses. In practice of course there is no such thing as 'the masses', only different groups that serve as pawns for various factions, all of whom may claim to have the masses behind them.

To judge from the steady drumfire of campaigns against bureaucracy since the early days of the regime none of the devices to humanize, purify, or mitigate the effects of bureaucracy has had much in the way of tangible results. It is somewhat curious that the Chinese Communists seem never to have considered one device widely used in the Israeli kibbutz (and often voiced in leftist circles elsewhere) to inhibit the growth of a bureaucratic caste: the frequent rotation of the duties of an administrative office among members of the people. The puzzle dissipates, however, on inspection of the concrete situation. Rotation in office works only where the duties of an office can be learned in a fairly short space of time, say a month or less for rotation of the job once a year. In other words the qualifications for the post have to be widespread among the population. If the main qualifications are political reliability and technical expertise, Communist Party leaders in China and elsewhere are likely to assume, by and large correctly, that these qualifications are scarce. Their scarcity in turn rules out any rotation in office.

One difference between political controls in the Soviet Union and China is that the controls in China penetrate more deeply. For China I have found almost no sign of the little enclaves where people, especially intellectuals, could wall themselves off and lead something like 'normal' lives, a condition that existed even under Stalin's rule in Russia. Under Mao by contrast the individual was often inserted into a small face-to-face group whose pressure assured at least outward conformity to the Party line of the moment. Even when several members of the group had their own doubts about what the regime was doing or demanding, the collective act of 'working over' a temporarily deviant and soon penitent member rapidly produced the desired results. What has happened to these practices since the death of Mao is not yet clear.

Turning now to the structure of inequality in China we find some broad similarities to the Soviet Union. At the top are the high political leaders whose position gives them special access to palatial homes, fine foods, and the other material goods that make civilization not only bearable but enjoyable. At the bottom are poor peasants in remote and infertile corners of China who lead a life of toil, close to starvation. There are also important differences from the Soviet Union. In China the main inequality is between the privileged (and often subsidized) city dwellers and the unprivileged dwellers in the countryside. This difference is the result of deliberate policy. To prevent the rise of an urban slum-dwelling population with all its consequences of increased crime, and also because the authorities did not wish to invest scarce resources to expand urban housing, transportation, and other facilities, the Chinese Communists in effect prohibited peasants from migrating into the cities. They could do this effectively through their control of jobs and ration cards. In recent times, however, they have been much less successful in preventing the return to their urban families of youths packed off to distant rural areas, after the Cultural Revolution sputtered out. The cities benefited from this policy while poverty and disguised unemployment mounted in the countryside, much as Marxists have told us it does in backward countries when capitalist industry destroys the demands for the products of native artisans.

There are signs, however, that this distinction between city dwellers and peasants may begin to blur as quite a number of peasants become rich under Deng's variant of a New Economic Policy. The main thrust of these post-Maoist reforms, discussed in some detail in the last part of Chapter 4, is toward making China a meritocracy. That is, people are to be rewarded in accord with their performance on the job, not for their political virtue or past services to the revolution. The government has also taken some hesitant steps toward a pricing policy that will reveal how well or how badly economic units are performing. At present, prices tell next to nothing about costs.

There is hardly any reason to doubt that these reforms are necessary if China is some day to become a modern industrial power. The real questions are, can the reforms take hold and become effective? Will the population at large accept them? Opposition can be expected from several sources: (1) bureaucrats who see their jobs disappearing with the reduction of economic controls and who also fear a general unraveling of socialism—after all socialism *is* controls; (2) doctrinaire radicals; (3) urban workers who see a threat to their job-security and relatively good wages; (4) military officers discontented at the sharp reduction of the military budget and the military establishment for the sake of capital investment in other areas. If these groups came together, which is not all that likely, their collective opposition could make the reforms founder. If the reforms do not raise the standard of living noticeably, that too would be the end of them. Fortunately there has been progress on that score already, especially in the countryside, even if large patches of extreme poverty remain. The most likely outcome, I suspect, is a compromise between the forces of modernizing reform and the revolutionary-bureaucratic status quo. Unfortunately for China the compromise could take the form in which most of the modernizing reform was in the showcase of speeches and symbolic acts while most of the sluggish bureaucratic structure remained intact and its behaviour unchanged. For more than two thousand years the inhabitants of China have coped with government by a moralizing élite. Both members of the élite and ordinary inhabitants are used to giving smiling assent to the day's edifying messages and promises as they go through life's familiar routines as best they can.

The final chapter is not a conventional set of conclusions in the sense of a concise restatement of findings presented earlier. Instead it is an attempt to explore the meaning of these findings in terms of a commitment to reducing human misery. Since any such effort must have a considerable speculative component, brevity will at least reduce the chances of making unfounded assertions. Since the chapter itself is short, a brief mention of some major points will do. The juxtaposition of the USA, the USSR, and China for comparative purposes draws attention to the fact that each regime arose in opposition to its historical predecessor in an attempt to create a less unjust and unequal society. For different reasons all three societies have displayed a generalized reluctance to accept hierarchy, authority, and inequality. There are, on the other hand, marked differences in the way each has tried to cope with the tensions between ideals and the apparent necessity for authority and inequality. Tyranny in socialist societies and unemployment under liberal capitalism have, along with other factors, discredited both socialism and capitalism, though a substantial degree of attachment does of course remain. With the apparent failure of secular solutions to political and economic misery, and the alleged moral and intellectual failures of modern science, there has been a return to religion. Despite some contrary trends there has been a marked growth of chauvinist fundamentalism in many parts of the world. It is as obvious in the United States as in Islamic countries or India. Nor is fundamentalism the only virulently anti-rationalist current. One can see very similar currents, including an ethical justification of violence, on the fringes of the environmentalist movement or among some anti-vivisectionists.

As old ghosts revive—ones that nineteenth-century optimists thought were exorcised for good—the prospect for a free and rational society, in any possible sense of this expression, becomes dim once more. But who summoned these ghosts and why?

2

THE USA

1 *Historical sources of authority and inequality*

AT the start it may be useful to give a very brief sketch of some major historical factors that have determined the shape of authority and social inequality in capitalist and socialist societies. One factor is a body of doctrines, such as Thomas Jefferson's synthesis of Enlightenment theories, and their intellectual successors which later crystallized in Marxism–Leninism. Such social theories present a continuing diagnosis of social ills—including what one should and should not see as an ill—and a series of remedies for them. Though the remedies seldom work, by providing a framework for understanding human society, the theories have a very powerful influence on the policies of rulers. Political and social doctrines are of course anything but static. Political and intellectual leaders are continually reinterpreting them in response to the realization that they do not work very well, if at all. Sometimes the reinterpretations are a matter of dispute. At other times, as we shall see, key aspects of doctrine can be reinterpreted out of existence or set aside as values deserving lip service on specified ritual occasions.

A second set of factors arises from the requirements of industrialization, that is: (a) how to get the resources to build machines; (b) how to put the machines together with men and women to turn out huge numbers of new products; and (c) how to distribute the products among the general population. The third set is the context of international relations. This context can often be the main factor that determines whether or not an historically new type of society can get started.[1] Thus French intervention was crucial in the American Revolution while the absence of powerful Western intervention was crucial to the success of the Russian and Chinese Communist Revolutions.

Like the realm of ideas, including religious ideas, and the realm of economic institutions, the realm of politics—or the organization and disorganization of authority—displays considerable autonomy. Often the best explanation of some form of political behaviour is to be found in another piece of political behaviour. Thus the politics of any given country are a simultaneous response to the international context with its threats and challenges and to domestic economic problems, both being perceived through the foggy lenses of a received doctrine. The main point to emerge from these brief comments is that every major country faces similar problems and issues in the course of industrialization—including whether to industrialize at all. Over time there are changes in the nature of the problems and the feasibility of the solutions. But it is the solutions that differ more than the problems. Prior traditions and social institutions, together with the international context, largely determine the solutions. These range from authoritarian capitalist through liberal capitalist to socialist.

2   Antagonism toward authority in the USA

Turning now to the United States and beginning with a look at current doctrines, the first impression is likely to be the absence of any single body of ideas that could channel political or more general discussion about the character of this society. There is no single or predominant remedy for American ills, not even one that could be widely attacked because it seems factually mistaken and morally wrong. (Factual and moral errors do not necessarily have anything to do with one another.) Instead one sees a rank profusion of incompatible ideas. They range from the most nonsensical forms of nativist or romantic anti-rationalism—which have been on the increase lately—through pragmatic realism to highly abstruse forms of rationalism and idealism (as in John Rawls, *A Theory of Justice* (Cambridge, Mass., 1971)). Yet this apparent confusion may conceal significant recurring themes. To find out we shall have to look more closely at patterns of social behaviour as well as ideas.

For a long time there has been a noticeable reluctance to accept any kind of authority in the United States. No individual or office is immune to criticism, sometimes quite savage criticism and abuse. In the absence of an hereditary aristocracy Americans do not have the habit of deference that has been ascribed to the British. Americans have heroes, mainly figures in sports and entertainment, with a scattering in space exploration and other dramatic areas of science. But they lack comparable figures of authority. Well below the level of national political leadership one finds the same reluctance to accept authority. Some thirty years ago a distinguished anthropologist observed that bosses, politicians, teachers, and 'big shots' were all accepted only at a discount in American society in so far as their positions implied authority.[2] More recently there has appeared a substantial body of evidence from opinion polls indicating a loss of confidence in political and economic leadership since that time. The decline began during the war in Vietnam and has continued since the end of that war.[3] Such a loss of trust implies a further deterioration of authority, since authority implies trust in those who command.

In any modern society perhaps the best index to the acceptance of the government's authority is the population's willingness to pay taxes and pay them honestly. On this score American behaviour has deteriorated sharply in the course of about one generation. Twenty-five years ago it was possible for American scholars knowledgeable about such matters to make fun of the Italians and the French for cheating on their income taxes. Nowadays American cheating is reported to be, if anything, worse than that in France and Italy. American cheating is by no means confined to criminal circles. The Internal Revenue Service estimates that for every dollar not paid on illegal income, nine dollars are not paid on legal income. Unreported legal income reached 250 billion dollars in 1981. By now it is considerably higher. What the Treasury loses from legal and illegal loopholes would almost balance the budget, if it could be collected.[4]

It is worthwhile to try to locate somewhat more precisely the time when this recent loss of authority took place and the causes of this failure. There are good reasons for holding that it derived from the disintegration during the 1960s and 1970s of the New Deal coalition forged by Franklin Roosevelt in 1932. Nearly forty years ago Hans Morgenthau remarked that if one studied this coalition in a seminar, one would conclude that it was an impossibility. The coalition was put together with urban workers, recently enfranchised urban immigrants, and intellectuals (together the sources of its liberal reformist wing), along with a broad spectrum of the then rural South with a substantial reactionary component, and other discontented farmers in the Mid-West, the whole topped off with a numerically small but fairly influential set of business leaders who saw no other way out of the Depression. The New Deal did not put an end to the Depression. The boom of the Second World War did that. Nevertheless the coalition was successful for a long time, from 1932 to the 1960s and beyond. Its main policies were economic growth, limited encouragement of unions, and social welfare expenditures at home for the sake of equity and social peace. Abroad its policies emphasized the support of preferably but not necessarily liberal regimes as a bulwark against Communist expansion and in order to create a favourable climate for American interests. American efforts to promote European recovery through the Marshall Plan may have represented the high point in the success of the coalition's policies. Prior to Reagan, Republican presidents did not stray far from these policies, except in their rhetoric.

As early as the 1950s, difficulties had begun to set in, each one intensifying the others. It became apparent that perpetual economic growth would not solve all social problems. Instead it created new ones, such as poisoning the water and the atmosphere. Workers rapidly became hostile to the environmentalists, whom they saw as upper class do-gooders cutting off their opportunities for fun, money, and big cars just at the point when workers were starting to make enough money to enter the consumer society. Welfare spending grew without producing peace or social order. Blacks rioted over long-standing grievances that suddenly seemed legitimate to many middle-class whites, especially young ones. In the cities crime increased and seemed to become more violent and vicious.

The most serious shock to the liberal establishment, however, came from foreign affairs in the form of the war in Vietnam. Many opponents of this conflict called it the Liberals' War. On the Asian continent, unlike the situation in Europe, there were no dependable democratic allies for the United States to support against a military and revolutionary, as well as nationalist, communist offensive. Before long the government in Washington found itself fighting a war that was increasingly unpopular at home and without real prospect of victory. After a long search for a diplomatic fig leaf to cover its withdrawal, the United States eventually just abandoned the field. Thus for the first time in its history, defeat in war came to the United States. Defeat as such, on the other hand, was not so important. The significance of the war lay in the way it made so many Americans from all classes and occupations ask searching and painful questions about their own society and the authorities that ruled them. The mood of guilt has by now of course subsided. But questions once asked seldom vanish altogether. Instead they remain in the form of psychic sore spots that may burst into inflammation under renewed pressure.

The war in Vietnam intensified latent pressures toward inflation because the war was financed mainly through borrowing instead of by taxes. Needless to say, the effect of inflation on authority is to introduce elements of apparent—or should one say visible—injustice all through the society. The traditional connection between effort and reward is twisted out of shape. Those with scarce goods and scarce skills reap inflated rewards, while those working for sticky wages or lacking goods for sale see their standard of living deteriorate and their savings evaporate. According to some economists a major cause of inflation has been the invisible handshake between unions and business executives. This is another aspect of the search for social peace. Rather than undergo an expensive strike, business leaders tacitly or openly grant their unions a hefty wage increase and pass the costs along to the consumer in the form of higher prices. Union leaders know what is going on and are, by and large, happy with the arrangement. The invisible handshake can work only in good times with an expanding economy. Another major cause of inflation was of course the sudden rise in the price of oil. No amount of American authority could do much about this rise. But rather unexpectedly the workings of the market have greatly diminished the power of the oil exporters and greatly moderated inflation. Whether it will recur under the present administration's policy of no money for social peace and transfer payments—except for Social Security and its powerful constituents— and billions for defence, remains to be seen. A government that promises not to tax its population while it takes resources away from the market would seem headed for another burst of inflation. All this has taken place under a rhetoric of nostalgia for individual independence and virtue. Because this rhetoric appeals to the discontents of many little people, it serves to legitimate current forms of authority and current policies.[5]

At this point it is necessary to enter a general caution. Like any other attitude, attitudes toward authority take very different forms of expression in different circumstances. Over long periods of time American culture displays a strong current of generalized disobedience. Simultaneously the government acts semi-paralysed by conflicting interests. Yet the paralysis and rejection of authority can vanish for a time in the case of war or unusually severe economic stress. Then those in authority are expected to act swiftly and without challenge. On his inauguration President Franklin D. Roosevelt closed all the banks in the country for four days. Nobody had any money except that in purse or pocket. Then Congress convened in a special session to make the President's behaviour legal.

A much more unsavoury episode took place shortly after the Japanese attack that forced American entry into the Second World War. On the advice of the military, President Roosevelt ordered all persons of Japanese descent, including American citizens, away from the West Coast. They were sent either to enemy alien camps or to detention camps if they were citizens, though a few were permitted to return home to other parts of the country if they had a home. There was no serious challenge to this executive decree, though some indignation arose after the war. Thus, despite their general dislike of authority, Americans accept it willingly enough in what they perceive as an emergency, especially if the authority is to affect someone else. To give one last example, there are frequent demands to give more authority to the police in order to stop the increase in crime.

Several reasons for this dislike of authority are apparent. There may be a substratum of basic human nature behind it. Authority implies restraint, and restraint is generally unpleasant even if socially necessary. But such generalizations cannot tell us anything about specific American attitudes toward authority. These are the precipitate of historical experience. Early in their history Americans experienced British authority in forms they defined as arbitrary and then rejected by force of arms.[6] When they established their own form of government in a written constitution, they tried to make sure that the new government could not act in the same arbitrary and 'tyrannical' fashion as the British allegedly had done. On this score they were rather successful. The famous division of powers between executive, legislative, and judicial branches of government is not a myth of political science textbooks. One has only to look at a daily newspaper to realize that these three branches are continually at each other's throats and that policy emerges as a compromise among them. These three branches are of course not the only contestants in the political arena. There are the major interest groups of industry, labour, and the farmers, each composed of a series of subgroups, and a host of other special interest groups, such as professionals (especially the medical lobbies), blacks, ethnic minorities, the elderly, feminists, homosexuals, and many others. Political parties try to focus all these groups and forces for their own purposes, mainly getting and holding offices. Regional alignments form out of the differential distribution of interest groups in various parts of the country. Meanwhile, the contest among interest groups and regions powers the contest among the three branches of government.

From this description one might infer that nearly all Americans are

passionately if selfishly interested in politics. Nothing could be further
from the truth. Poll after poll has found a large mass of people who
know next to nothing about politics and care even less. For the most
part, interest groups are like awkward swimmers lashing the surface of
the waters to create a little current moving in the direction they want.
Meanwhile the depths of the ocean remain undisturbed.

One should not overemphasize the anarchic trend in American
politics for another reason. The founding fathers of the Constitution,
who were part of a brilliant but short-lived patrician élite, wanted a
government with enough authority to protect property and serve as a
'barrier against domestic faction and insurrection'.[7] This theme of the
proper role of authority in protecting property was to remain highly
influential for a long time. It was only from the time of the New Deal
that concern for the welfare of those who had no property pushed this
theme toward the background of public concerns. Nevertheless one
can make a good case for the thesis that the strategy of the New Deal
was to preserve the institutions of private property by requiring those
who had most of it to make some sacrifices for the benefit of the rest.

The relatively equal distribution of property prior to industrialization also had consequences for attitudes about authority and equality.
The latter we will discuss shortly. To avoid misunderstanding it is
necessary to emphasize that there were substantial pockets of wealth
in towns and cities and that a plantation oligarchy grew up in the South
during the nineteenth century. But property, especially landed
property, was distributed fairly equally in comparison with countries
where a nobility owned the lion's share of the land. Together with the
frontier that created an emphasis on self-reliance, the existence of a
large class of independent farmers and artisans supported an ethic of
individualism under which each man could claim to be as good as
anyone else. And where a man feels as good as anybody else—a
sentiment by no means dead even today—he will be reluctant to grant
anybody else authority over him.

By way of provisional summing up we can point to at least three
sources of antagonism to authority that were at work in American
society before the advent of big industry. One was the experience of
British rule that was felt to be arbitrary and capricious. Another was the
experience of frontier society, where the government was remote and
the individual depended on his own resources. Finally, nineteenth-
century American society was one with a widespread distribution of
property that promoted an individualist ethic and resistance to author-

ity. All of these forces have ceased to operate and did so more than a century ago. Yet they still have echoes in American thinking that reverberate, as new sources of hostility to authority put in an appearance.

3 Effects of the rise of big business

The advent of big industry, from the 1880s on, fundamentally altered the nature of authority and inequality in the United States. Big industry, or more properly big business, which includes big commerce and transportation such as the railroads, introduced command–obedience relationships in the form of bureaucracy. The railroads, however, were the first to introduce administrative hierarchies by the late 1850s, in order to co-ordinate the expeditious and moderately safe movement of freight and passengers over their far-flung network of tracks. By 1870 bureaucratic systems were well in place on the railroads and by 1900 in large manufacturing and commercial firms.[8] Furthermore, through the creation of a wealthy business élite and a large class of wage earners with little or no property, the advent of big business greatly magnified economic inequalities. Yet anti-authoritarian egalitarianism did by no means disappear even if deprived of its economic base. As a disembodied ideal it has long energized the laments of social critics and reformers who surface whenever some form of injustice appears, which occurs nearly all the time.

One possible reason for the continued life of this disembodied ideal is the historical fact that American big business managed to import a substantial portion of its 'proletariat' through open immigration. In turn, ethnic divisions within the working class helped to inhibit the growth of a socialist challenge to the rule of big business. Thus there was no powerful political organization to hammer home the mythical nature of anti-authoritarian egalitarianism or to present a plausible alternative to the status quo. People were free to believe in these ideals without fully realizing they were a form of romantic nostalgia. Indeed, under President Reagan, this romantic nostalgia has become a political programme.

In the United States bureaucracy arose mainly from the requirements of big industry, and only much later, at the time of the New Deal, from the requirements of running a big government.[9] To be sure the federal government had acquired wide powers of control over business during the First World War. But the controls were put out of action with the end of the war, giving business free rein to generate what was hoped to be a permanently rising prosperity. In contrast to the origins of bureaucracy in America, let us recall the sharply different sources in other parts of the world. In Prussia, for example, bureaucracy arose long before the coming of industry. Its source lay in the military and a militarized government. Earlier, in the ancient Near East, the late Roman Empire, and Imperial China, bureaucracy had already put in an appearance. As such, therefore, it is not at all a feature peculiar to industrial societies or societies attempting to industrialize rapidly. Nevertheless, today bureaucracy and hostility to bureaucracy are the most important traits shared by capitalist and socialist societies.

4 *Bureaucratic behaviour*

Bureaucracy derives from the need of a society's leaders to co-ordinate or control the actions of a large number of people or a large number of activities. In the case of the railroads just mentioned, administrative hierarchies arose to ensure that a large number of railroad cars reached their separate destinations as rapidly as possible. The formal organization of a bureaucracy is one of a hierarchy with command–obedience relationships from top to bottom. The higher the position in the hierarchy the greater the number of individuals subject to that authority. In modern Western bureaucracies the scope of authority is supposedly limited to activities connected with the job, that is, the task the bureaucracy is intended to perform. A railroad administrator supposedly does not inquire into the private life of a switchman, unless the switchman shows up drunk for work rather too often.

In practice there is a great deal of deviation from the strict model of command–obedience relationships. Authority is by no means strictly limited to matters pertaining to the job. Many a large American company has dress codes for its desk-bound employees, presumably to ensure that the company maintains a sufficiently dignified public image. In recent years too there has been quite a bit of public discussion about what is expected of the corporate wife, that is, the wife of an executive in a large firm.

While there are signs like these of an extension of bureaucratic authority beyond its proper realm, there is evidence to demonstrate a much more important tendency toward the restriction of superior authority by the lower ranks. In practice, a bureaucracy seldom resembles its organizational chart, with its lines of authority flowing downward into little boxes representing people with different tasks.

Instead, it resembles a burgeoning series of largely independent and competing cells, all anxious for access to higher authority and more funds. Meanwhile each cell works out its own informal but effective rules of behaviour for its own members. These rules control the division of labour and methods of work within the unit, such as, for example, what facts out of all those required must actually be put on the records, and how the records will be filed. These informal work rules also serve as a barrier against undue curiosity and interference by higher administrative authorities. At the same time higher authorities continually seek to penetrate the bureaucratic cells beneath them for the sake of their own authority.

Sometimes it seems a wonder that bureaucracies ever accomplish anything. Leaving aside for the moment the elements of enthusiasm and terror that characterize newly created bureaucracies in the early stages of socialism, we can inquire into the exercise of authority in Western, and primarily American, administrative systems. These are not at all the faceless impersonal organizations described by Kafka. Instead they are rather cheery, even toward clients and ordinary citizens a great deal of the time, and in their workings very personal. An American administrator seldom tries to oppose or overrule the informal organization of his subordinates. To do that would be to court disaster for his own reputation and career since subordinates can see to it that nothing succeeds for an administrator they dislike. Instead, he works through the informal organization by disregarding minor infractions of rules. Often enough, rule-breaking is essential to getting a job done. By doing this and protecting his staff from the depredations of other segments of the bureaucracy, he earns the loyalty of his staff. This loyalty may then pay off in willingness to do extra work when a rush job comes along. Then the administrator can get credit for a job well done.[10]

In order to learn the mood of his own staff, as well as threats and opportunities in the larger bureaucratic environment, an administrator spends a great deal of time gathering personal information. That is one explanation for the apparently endless round of staff meetings. At staff meetings lower ranks meet with higher ranks, and the prestige of a lower official derives in part from the highest ranking individual who comes to the same meeting. Frequent rounds of coffee are part of American staff meetings. Even if they make few important decisions, they provide information about moods and problems elsewhere in the bureaucracy, and sometimes even the world at large, revealing what

policies are likely to work and which ones likely to fail. The coffee too
has its sociological benefits, since the lavatory is often an important
place for exchanging news among American males.

Bureaucracies vary considerably of course in accord with the functions they perform and the political milieu in which they operate. For
instance, a useful study of managerial hierarchies in five countries—
Yugoslavia, the kibbutzim of Israel, the USA, Austria, and Italy—
found sharp hierarchical gradients everywhere, except possibly in
Yugoslavia, where the authors regarded their data as unreliable. But
there were important differences. The kibbutz plants showed the least
steep gradient of authority and the Italian ones the steepest.[11]

Here I would like to draw attention to two factors that have a
powerful influence on systems of authority under both capitalist and
socialist systems. One is the level of skill among subordinates. A high
level of skill creates tendencies toward equality. The other is the
degree of danger or threat in the environment. For groups above the
size of face-to-face or first-name relationships, danger generally promotes a demand for discipline and obedience or, in other words,
organized inequality.

First let us look more closely at the role of skill. Command–
obedience relationships are at a minimum where the task requires a
high level of skill and the workers have this skill. In this situation the
relationships between the superior and the work force is primarily one
of co-operative problem solving. To keep the worker's respect the
supervisor has to know as much as the worker, and it is better if he
knows even more. Direct orders are kept to an absolute minimum.
Otherwise a worker may balk and simply refuse to do a job. An
unwelcome order is an affront to his self-respect, and especially so if it
comes from someone unfamiliar with the technical requirements of the
task. At times certain linguistic conventions may spring up that serve to
conceal the command–obedience relationships between people behind
the technical imperatives of the job. Thus, a shipyard foreman,
instructing an experienced carpenter on how to make up and install a
piece of cabinet work in a tight corner of a ship's cabin, will use
anthropomorphic expressions: 'This piece of wood wants to go here.
The other one wants to go over there.' The carpenter understands that
it is his job to shape the pieces of wood very accurately so that they will
'go there'.

The opposite kind of situation is likely to arise where the plant
employs a large number of unskilled workers, often migrants from the

countryside or immigrants from abroad. In such a situation it may be necessary to supervise every move of workers who have a very limited comprehension of what is happening or why. There is likely to be a high ratio of foremen to workers, and the foremen are likely to be brusque and impatient. Actually, much of the discipline comes from the machines which determine what human operations are necessary and the pace of these operations. This was the case in the early textile plants and remains the case today wherever the assembly-line exists. By 1973, however, assembly-line jobs probably came to less than two per cent of all the jobs in the United States.[12] This extreme form of authority relationship has become a quite minor form. There are reasons for suspecting that its importance may decline even further. Nowadays, when an employer becomes faced with a work force that seems sullen, inefficient, expensive, and militant, the employer turns to automation and robots if at all possible. Problems of control over human beings in this way are transformed into problems of control over more and more complicated machines.

Now let us turn to the effects of physical danger. As military discipline the world over shows, danger intensifies authority and increases the importance of command–obedience relationships. Even a passenger ship at sea is no democracy. All this is obvious to the point of banality. I think it has to be modified by taking into account the informal organization that always exists among subordinates. When a real emergency strikes in the form of an enemy attack or a bad storm at sea, the commanding officer is heavily dependent on what the men under his command will do. To a great extent they have to know what to do themselves and be able to do it fast. That capacity in turn depends on their own informal organization and division of labour. A good commanding officer is one who recognizes this situation and works with and through the informal organization rather than against it. In a paternalist fashion he will tolerate minor infractions of regulations in return for loyal and effective support in emergency. He will also try to get to know those under his command in other ways, treating them like individual human beings, rather than automata. Where that occurs, men often respect strictness in other areas closely related to a shared task or mission. Thus, even in the most strictly hierarchical organizations, there is a tendency to soften the sharper contours of authority.

5   *Differences between capitalist and socialist bureaucracies*

Here it is appropriate to ask what might be the most important
differences between bureaucracy in a liberal capitalist democracy and
bureaucracy in a socialist country. One difference is so obvious that we
need spend little time on it, even though the difference is very
important. In a liberal capitalist society the central government does
not try to control every aspect of social life from a single centre through
bureaucratic means. The liberal capitalist government is not expected
to do this. Intervention is expected only when enough people complain
about an 'intolerable' situation or when sufficiently powerful interests
claim they need assistance. A socialist society, on the other hand,
attempts to organize the thinking and the behaviour of the entire
population around specified goals. The pretence is maintained that the
masses are enthusiastic in pursuit of the goal. But practically everybody
realizes that the enthusiasm is mainly a useful fiction, useful, that is,
for those in charge.

The other major difference is this: under capitalism economic
inequality generates inequalities in social esteem and, less directly,
inequalities in authority. The rich do not run the state. They are too
busy making money or enjoying themselves. But, by and large, the state
has tried to find policies that will attract votes *and* be acceptable to
business leaders, a search that is not always a stunning success. Finally,
being rich has become quite an asset for a political career in the United
States. Under socialism all this is reversed: economic inequalities and
inequalities in social esteem come out of differences in political
authority.

In both systems, however, the higher political and economic administrators serve at the pleasure and discretion of somebody else.
Appointed supposedly for their performance and promise, high
administrators are exposed to intrigue, demotion, and dismissal. On
this score they turn out to be not so unequal after all. Hereditary
aristocrats were rather more secure in their privileges.

At this point in the discussion we glimpse a major break in the
continuity of human civilization that has had profound consequences
for forms of authority and social inequality. Before the coming of the
industrial revolution the chief way to increase wealth was by overt or
disguised compulsion. One just took things by means of conquest or
forced the underlying population in one's own country to turn over
more in the form of dues and taxes. Merchants there were of course.

They increased the flow of goods by moving them from one place to another where there was a demand for them. But merchants only moved goods. They did not produce them.

There were some exceptions. Agricultural yields grew as uncultivated lands were cleared and techniques of agriculture improved. The Cistercians, for example, are famous for their contributions to both forms of improvement, achieved mainly during the twelfth century. Manufactures began to grow as early as the sixteenth century. Nevertheless there was no drastic change in the situation before the coming of modern industry, a transformation clearly under way only by about the middle of the nineteenth century. Only then did it make practical sense to advise men and nations not to steal in order to become rich and powerful. Better ways had become apparent. With the help of machines one could set up an ever more abundant flow of goods, and services. There have, of course, been many besides Marx who have been sceptical about this newfangled and allegedly hypocritical bourgeois morality. My impression is that suspicion may be highest in the poorer countries with their expropriation of groups that have nothing to expropriate. There are also abundant signs that many people in search of wealth and profit prefer to use tried and true methods like fraud instead of financially risky ones, such as turning out serviceable products. Still these qualifications do not, so far as I can see, alter the fundamental fact that there has been a change in the system of production and in the moral principles of inequality sustaining this system.

As befitted a relatively static economic order with limited opportunities for improving one's situation either collectively or individually, pre-industrial justifications of inequality generally put a heavy stress on supposedly innate qualities. Religious doctrines justified inequality and helped to explain the distribution of moral qualities and defects among the quite visibly distinguishable strata of the population. Supposedly innate qualities came to be thought of as hereditary. A high-born person had certain privileges, such as the right to expect deference from social inferiors, the right to command troops in wartime, the right to certain forms of material support produced by the work of peasants, etc., simply because one was born an aristocrat.

There were, of course, important exceptions. Chinese society generated a bureaucracy theoretically open to merit, some two thousand years ago, although in practice the ownership of landed property played a major role. In the West the Catholic Church also provided a way, many centuries ago, for intelligent young men from poor or undistinguished backgrounds to achieve influential posts, especially if they displayed what would now be called 'executive talents'. In the light of these two major exceptions it may be too much to consider the transformation of inequality as being from one justified in terms of hereditary qualities to one based on merit and specific forms of competence. Nevertheless, such a change did occur, amid bloodshed and suffering. It continues today despite efforts to bring it to a halt. A real meritocracy may be impossible to live with because it offers no consolation for failure. Since the belief systems of civilized societies as different as the Hindu caste system and advanced liberal Christianity devote a great deal of attention to accounting for failure in ways inoffensive to the victim, we may guess that the need for such comfort is widespread and deep-rooted. We seem unable to face our own incompetence and failures any better than our inevitable death.

6 *Inequality in the USA*

To return to the American scene, the American Revolution opened with a blast against the whole idea of noble birth. The Declaration of Independence proclaimed as a self-evident truth the allegation that all men were created equal. It said nothing about women. And it said nothing about blacks.[13] Without time to discuss sexual and racial inequalities in any detail here, I would like to emphasize that both are very live issues in American society today, with racial discrimination the more acute one. Finally, the Declaration of Independence says nothing specific about what does or should happen to men after they are created. Presumably some aspects of equality should remain. Otherwise there would have been no point to saying anything about equality in the first place. But to judge from later discussion and practice, certain forms of inequality were to be expected and were morally acceptable. Equality came to mean equality of opportunity. All men should start the race of life from the same position, without unfair advantages or disadvantages. It is hardly necessary to point out that in its opposition to inherited wealth or inherited social advantages this is a utopian position for a complex 'civilized' society. After the race had started, men were expected to run at different speeds in search of wealth, fame, and comfort.[14]

As long as no one cheated, there was supposedly nothing wrong with big prizes going to some of the runners while others dropped out from sloth or exhaustion and got nothing. In practice, there was a huge amount of cheating and corruption, right from the beginning. Profiteers and speculators of the type who cornered the supply of shoes and warm clothing for the revolutionary army were, in George Washington's opinion, more dangerous than the entire military might of Great Britain.[15] From a comparative historical standpoint, the American image of society as essentially a race for material goods seems a bit peculiar, to say the least. But, until quite recently, there have been very few to suggest that there might be better things people could do with their time. For that matter, contemporary criticism of the passion for material goods comes in large measure from romantic rebels in easy circumstances.

Despite the cheating and speculation, for more than three generations after the Declaration of Independence had proclaimed that men were born equal, no great inequalities were apparent in the United States. In the 1830s, according to James Bryce, 'there were no great fortunes in the United States, few large ones, and no poverty'. By the time his *American Commonwealth* reached a second edition in 1891, both gigantic fortunes and poverty were plain for all to see.[16] These inequalities began to take shape after the Civil War as a consequence of the spurt in industrial growth that began after 1865. They have been with us ever since and show no sign of disappearing despite high income taxes, inheritance taxes, and rapidly rising transfer payments, such as welfare and social security. In 1965 government transfer payments were 37.6 billion dollars or five per cent of a gross national product of 691.1 billion. By 1983 these transfer payments had multiplied over ten times to reach 389.3 billion dollars. They came to eleven per cent of a GNP that had meanwhile risen almost five times to become 3304.8 billion dollars.[17]

Even these large transfer payments have not eliminated poverty. Nor should we expect them to. The conception of what constitutes poverty continually rises to include more and more goods and services, as the general standard of living in the United States keeps on rising. As an astringent economist has pointed out, a perpetually rising standard of living guarantees that there will always be poverty.[18] Furthermore, as Stanley Lebergott has also shown, even a confiscatory redistribution of income would provide no more than trivial help for the poor. By his calculations, carried out shortly before 1976, if the state confiscated all incomes above $25,000 a year, the poor would get at the most only $350 apiece. The poor would get that amount only if the state transferred all of this new revenue to the poor. If, on the other hand, the money went into the general coffers of the treasury and was spent in the same proportions as previous revenues, the poor would only get $12 apiece.[19] These observations show that those who find the juxtaposition of enormous riches and squalid poverty in America morally obscene cannot count on a mere redistribution to accomplish anything. Somehow they would have to bring about a reordering of American social structure and values. By definition, radicals want to do that anyway. At the same time these observations bring water to the conservative mill by showing the futility of efforts at redistribution by confiscating the 'excess' incomes of the rich.

With their stress on confiscatory redistribution these arguments may go too far. Together with other forces hard to specify, this rise in transfer payments has brought about a reduction in poverty that is by no means negligible. In 1959 18.1 per cent of the white population and 56.2 per cent of the black population were below the poverty line, as defined by the Social Security Administration and later revised by other government agencies. By 1982 the proportions had fallen to 12 per cent for whites and 35.6 for blacks. In slightly more human terms that means 23.5 million whites and 9.7 million black persons below the poverty line in 1982.[20] In 1983 the poverty line was set at an annual income of $5,061 for a single individual and $10,178 for a family or household of four.[21]

If the poor have not disappeared, neither have the rich, as one can see from a glance at the statistics on the distribution of income. At the bottom end in 1983 with incomes under $5,000 a year were 7.7 per cent of the white households and 21.1 per cent of the black households. At the other end of the scale were those receiving more than ten times as much or $50,000 a year and over. (According to *Business Week*, 9 May 1983, 84–5, the highest paid executive in the US in 1982 received a total of $1,806,000 or more than 36 times $50,000.) Of those receiving $50,000 a year and more, in 1983, there were 11.1 per cent of the white households and 3.1 per cent of the black households. Also in 1983, it is significant that the largest percentages of all households—17.7 per cent for whites and 11.7 per cent for blacks— fall in the income category one could consider quite well off, perhaps even upper middle class, that is, $25,000 to $34,999.[22]

A substantial portion of this upper middle class now comes from the rapidly increasing sector of professional and technical workers. Between 1960 and 1981 their numbers more than doubled, rising from 7,469,000 to 16,420,000. However, their proportion of the employed population rose only from 14.2 per cent in 1970 to 16.4 per cent in 1981. Still outnumbered by the blue-collar workers, the professional and technical workers are rapidly gaining on them. Though the blue-collar workers gained in absolute numbers from 24,057,000 in 1960 to 31,261,000 in 1981, their proportion of the employed population dropped from 35.3 per cent in 1970 to 31.1 per cent in 1981. By 1981 there were more than half as many professional and technical workers as there were blue-collar workers, whereas in 1960 the ratio was fewer than one to three.[23] For the most part, the professional and technical workers are the carriers of a belief in the beneficial effects of action by the federal government—very often their source of funds—and of new cosmopolitan, and somewhat permissive, tastes in leisure. Thus their culture acts corrosively on traditional and rural-based values, especially those that held saving and visible hard work (often physical) as perhaps the only morally acceptable bases for inequality.[24]

These statistics confirm and extend the results of common observation. To be sure, the United States is a land of sharp extremes in poverty and wealth. On the other hand, it is also a rich country with a substantial proportion of the people able to live in comfortable circumstances. Even a number of blacks (11.7 per cent in 1983) share now in the general prosperity. This distribution of income helps to explain the conservative tenor of American political life and the lack of response to demands for a complete overhaul of American institutions generated by the war in Vietnam. What is harder to explain is the tone of fearful crusading that conservatism has displayed when in power.

If the information to be gleaned about the upper middle class indicates a continuation of conservative stability, that is not necessarily the case with the middle class itself. Economists studying the figures on the size and earnings of this class have recently concluded, despite some differences in their statistical methods, that this class, supposedly the backbone of liberal capitalist democracy, has been shrinking for some time. It has lost a few members who have moved up to a richer stratum, and many more who have dropped down to a poorer level. Stephen J. Rose defined middle-income families as those with annual incomes of $11,500 to $27,400 in 1978 or $17,000 to $41,000 in 1983. In 1978 approximately 55 per cent of the population fell between the first set of boundaries. In 1983 the proportion between the second set of boundaries was only 42 per cent. In other words, there was a drop of 13 per cent in only five years. Of those who left the middle class, three-quarters suffered a decline in their standard of living. Only a quarter improved it.[25]

Using somewhat different figures and time periods, the well-known economist Lester C. Thurow reaches roughly similar conclusions, though in his figures the strength of the trends eroding the middle class appear less powerful. He uses as a range of incomes for middle-class households $15,100 and $25,200 in 1982. On this basis he finds that the middle-class declined from 28.2 per cent of the population in 1967 to 23.7 per cent 'now'—which might be any time between 1982 and 1984. In any case Thurow reports a drop of slightly under five percentage points for fifteen years as against Rose's drop of thirteen percentage points in only five years. Thurow further reported that about half of those who left the middle class rose above it and about half fell below. The size of the income groups above and below the middle class each increased by about two per cent. This is a trend in the direction of a bipolar distribution of income, with the rich clustering at one end and the poor at the other, as Thurow points out. But at only two per cent a year it would take quite a while for serious consequences to appear.[26]

Both economists agree in their assessment of the main causes for these trends. The economy, as Rose puts it succinctly, is creating high-income jobs in high technology industries and many lower paying service jobs for workers such as building custodians, cooks, waiters, and others. But the number of middle-income jobs in the automobile, steel, machinery, construction, and other manufacturing industries has fallen off sharply. To this Thurow adds a significant point. In his judgement, the unions in the industries that have now fallen off in production were in the past able to push wages up beyond the level warranted by the workers' skills, thereby creating, for a time, many middle-income jobs that are now ceasing to exist. Other factors too are important, such as jobs lost through the deterioration in the American position in international trade. This is not the occasion, however, to go into further detail. Because the findings of the two studies vary quite widely, I think it is a bit early to accept their pessimistic conclusions. They deserve attention, but not alarmed attention.

A few figures on the distribution of wealth will complete the picture of economic inequality in the United States. Wealth refers to what one has or possesses. Income refers to what comes in on a regular recurring basis. The accummulation of wealth in the contemporary world is possible of course only in a capitalist society. In a socialist society, where there is no private property in the means of production, it is almost out of the question to acquire wealth, though a few individuals, such as popular and officially approved writers, have managed to amass quite substantial sums. Figures on wealth in the US are harder to come by than those on income, perhaps because an individual's total assets only come to light at death. But there are some figures on the share of all wealth held by the richest one per cent. In 1929 it was 36.3 per cent or well over one-third of all wealth. By 1972 (the most recent year for available figures) their share had fallen, with some minor fluctuations during the interim, to 20.7 per cent or slightly over one-fifth. We also have some figures on the dollar value of assets held by all persons and by the top 0.5 per cent. The net worth of all persons in 1976 amounted to 4,596.8 billion dollars. Of these, the richest one-half per cent had a net worth of 659.6 billion dollars or 14.3 per cent of all wealth. There were 1.08 million very rich individuals in this top half per cent, as compared with 25 million below the poverty line in 1976 (and 35.3 million in 1983).[27] Contrary to popular impressions, a substantial body of evidence indicates that great riches do not last very long. Instead they are likely to be dissipated among wives, children, pleasures, and good works. There is a corresponding tendency for many members of the wealthiest group to be recruited from below, perhaps as much as forty to sixty per cent. In other words, the extremely rich do not constitute a self-perpetuating and exclusive oligarchy, at least not in the United States.[28]

There are at least two ways to explain the kinds of inequality just described. One is to show how and why society has created a set of unequally rewarded positions. The other is to take these unequally rewarded positions more or less for granted and find out how and why individuals in the society, in the course of their lives, become distributed among these positions.

The first explanation requires a recapitulation of the main features of capitalism, something I shall not attempt in any detail. Great wealth comes partly from the creation of wholly new industries, often by not very scrupulous entrepreneurs. There is also a process of industrial and financial concentration. In the course of competition larger firms drive little ones to the wall, either buying them out or letting them die. In a great many cases, big firms have little ones as satellite suppliers. Finally, there is the creation and disciplining of the industrial labour force, a mass of people with little or no property but with labour power to sell. The United States is unusual on this score in having imported

The USA

so much of its proletariat, first in the form of black slaves and much later in the form of white immigration. This set of forces created the combination of great wealth and severe poverty characteristic of capitalism. But, as pointed out above, capitalism also created a large middle class and a series of steps between the very rich and the very poor.

The best studies of the way people get to different occupations and levels of income in American society are those by Christopher Jencks and his associates. They are critical and interpretative reviews of survey data and, therefore, heavily statistical, though quite accessible to the non-specialist reader. Their general effect is to demolish, or at least diminish very sharply, the power of conventional explanations of inequality given by conservatives, liberals, and even some radicals. 'Neither family background, cognitive skills, education attainment, nor occupational status', Jencks asserts, 'explain much of the variation in men's incomes.' Comparing men who are identical in all these respects, he continues, 'we find only 12 to 15 per cent less inequality than among random individuals'.[29]

A later publication by Jencks and his associates presents some updated and slightly revised figures on some of these factors. Family background might explain 15–35 per cent of the variance in mature men's earnings.[30] Years of education were found to be correlated 0.38 to 0.49 with earnings. Put somewhat differently, education 'explained' about 55 per cent of true variance in occupation but only about 20 per cent of true variance in income.[31] Thus education appears as the only variable with substantial explanatory power, and then only in connection with the choice of occupation. But, as everyone knows, there is a wide range of earnings to be had, and education, as such, has very little to do with where an individual ends up on this range.

With all traditional explanations of inequality demolished, Jencks resorted in *Inequality* to luck. Luck covers such matters as whether a new superhighway has an exit near your restaurant, or whether you get a job in a firm that expands and promotes you instead of a firm that goes broke and leaves you with a set of unmarketable skills.[32] In the later publication he amplified and corrected his conception of luck. By my reading, luck then became another word for the structure of the economy and state of the business cycle, matters the individual could do nothing about even if he understood them and their local significance completely (which is very rarely the case). Nevertheless, this conception of luck is important because it brings us back to the structural and historical determinants of inequality emphasized in the first explanation. Because such factors are in part historical, they vary from case to case and between capitalist and socialist societies. But the overall results are broadly similar. They will appear in the next two chapters.

3

THE USSR

1 *Autocracy and totalitarianism*

STALINIST Russia was a totalitarian state, most of whose features remain standing today. The origins of Stalinist totalitarianism lie deep in the history of Tsarist autocracy. Before examining these connections it is necessary to spend a few moments on the meaning of the words 'totalitarian' and 'autocratic'. The word totalitarian is out of fashion now among many American scholars because of its connection with the cold war. Some see the term as mere pejorative epithet used to discredit the Soviet regime. As one who is keenly aware of crusading hypocrisy on both sides in the East–West conflict, I nevertheless find totalitarian a useful and meaningful term. It refers to a regime that tries, with considerable success, to control the whole range of human thought and action from a single centre for the purpose of achieving a total transformation of human behaviour in the direction of some allegedly higher goal.

The line between an autocratic and a totalitarian regime is, admittedly, at times thin and blurred. Peter the Great, for example, sounds like a totalitarian ruler in his efforts to westernize Russia by force. Yet in comparison with Stalin his efforts seem puny. They left the basic class structure and political system largely untouched. More generally, an autocratic regime lacks the will and the means to carry through a total revolution of the social order. So long as they do not constitute a perceived threat to the existing political authorities, many human activities under an autocracy are allowed to go their own way. In nineteenth-century Russia, literature reached one of the world's great peaks of creative originality, with no more than minor interference from the Tsarist censorship. Such freedom for literature and the arts was out of the question under Stalin. (According to a widely circulated joke, the only music permitted was what Stalin could whistle.)

The main similarities between autocracy, mainly a pre-industrial form of rule, and totalitarian dictatorship are fairly obvious. Both display a high concentration of power at the centre, perhaps more intense in the case of a totalitarian regime with its superior control of the means of transport, communication, and violence. Neither kind of regime tolerates opposition readily nor, when at the height of its power, refrains from cruelty and violence in crushing this opposition. The existence of semi-tolerated opposition is a sign of decay in either an old-fashioned autocracy or a modern totalitarian dictatorship.

2 Tsarist autocracy: liberal alternatives and their weakness

The habits of mind and social institutions forged in the course of history to support the Tsarist autocracy placed powerful obstacles in the way of any democratic and liberal resolution to the tensions Russian society faced in the late nineteenth and early twentieth centuries. Russian feudalism was sufficiently different from West European feudalism to make some authors doubt whether it deserves to be called feudalism at all. Without attempting to answer that question, it is sufficient to draw attention to the nature of the difference as perceived by the great historian Marc Bloch. In the West he saw 'reciprocity in unequal obligations' symbolized by the act of homage which thereby became a contract. All this was missing in Russia.[1] Another major difference was that Western feudalism early on generated the theory and practice of a right of resistance to royal authority.[2] Yet it would be very misleading to leave the impression that in the course of Russian history there were no indigenous movements that could have led toward a liberal and democratic outcome.[3] As the German historian Otto Hoetzsch pointed out, it is not in the least true that from the beginning Russia was a non-democratic, absolutist, and despotic state. There were in the Kievan period, in the tenth and eleventh centuries, democratic institutions of considerable importance. One was the assembly of clan elders, comparable to the Germanic *Thing*. Another was the *vetche* or popular assembly in the towns. But at an early date both fell victims to the power of the territorial princes.[4] Again much later, in the seventeenth century at the beginning of the Romanov dynasty, royal absolutism was temporarily weakened. The Tsar ruled in conjunction with a quasi-parliamentary gathering of leaders of the *Stände* or status groups. This gathering was known as the *zemskii sobor* (roughly, gathering of the land). Without the council of the nobility the Tsar could do nothing, and the *zemskii sobor* from time to time issued laws.[5] In time of course the Tsars recovered their power, which rested on superior control of the instruments of violence. In turn, so far as I can discern, this superiority of the means of violence stemmed from a general acceptance by the upper classes of a need for domestic tranquillity as well as the protection and extension of the Russian state.

These trends led to the firm establishment of a bureaucratic, military state that had further negative consequences for the prospects of a liberal democratic regime. It greatly inhibited the growth of a bourgeoisie, one of the most important prerequisites for a liberal democracy. Right up to the collapse of the Empire, most Russian cities were garrison towns and administrative centres, not foci for trading and manufacturing.[6] When a capitalist bourgeoisie did put in an appearance during the last half of the nineteenth century, compared to its English counterpart it was a weak and sickly thing. Both economically and politically it was heavily dependent on the Tsar's fickle favour.[7] On this score it is important to recognize the dilemma facing the Tsar. As early as the Crimean War, 1854–6, it had become plain that Russia needed an industrial base in order to modernize her antiquated military forces. But policy-makers feared industrial growth because of its potentially disruptive social and political consequences. It is hardly too much to claim that the Tsarist autocracy foundered on this dilemma in 1917.

One can trace a connection between the Tsarist autocracy and the Bolshevik dictatorship in the following manner. The Tsarist autocracy generated a revolutionary opposition because a democratic one was impossible. This revolutionary opposition took the form of Lenin's conspiratorial élite. Thus it was a mirror image of Tsarism. As the only effective way to fight Tsarism, the theory of a conspiratorial élite had far-reaching consequences. It formed the basis of the post-revolutionary organization of the Party, the Soviet State, and the Communist International. In my judgement all of these claims are true. But they convey partial truths that are, therefore, misleading.

3   *Early Bolshevik responses to the issues of authority and inequality*

There were contrary trends that require our attention. In 1903 Bolsheviks and Mensheviks alike, as good Marxists, still believed that Russia would have to pass through a capitalist and democratic phase before proceeding to a socialist revolution. Thus the Party declaration separated the ultimate socialist goal from the immediate one of a democratic republic. Two points in their democratic programme are quite striking in the light of what actually happened: (a) the inviolability of the person and the home; (b) unrestricted freedom of conscience, of speech, of the press, of association, and the right to strike.[8]

There is evidence showing that for Russian Marxists these goals had an appeal in their own right even if they were bourgeois freedoms, not socialist ones. At the same Party Congress in 1903 Plekhanov (not Lenin) asserted that the good of the revolution ought to be the supreme law of revolutionary activity, even if it meant temporary restrictions on democratic activities. Only one minor delegate supported Plekhanov. At that point there were shocked exclamations from the audience and cries, 'How about the inviolability of the person?'[9]

Such an episode reveals a general dilemma of which many Russian Marxists were keenly aware. On the one hand, they were trying to make a revolution on behalf of greater human freedom. On the other hand, success in making this revolution required a resort to means that would restrict, and could destroy, this freedom.

The theory of democratic centralism was one attempt to cope with this dilemma. The essence of the idea was summed up in a famous phrase of Lenin's, 'freedom in discussion—unity in action'. In other words, once an issue had been thrashed out within the Party and a decision reached by a majority vote at a Party Congress, or by the Central Committee in the interim between Congresses, all members were obliged to support the decision, no matter what their personal views might be. Failure to support the Party's official policy in word and deed was a very serious violation of Party discipline.[10] Thus democratic centralism was intended as a way of softening the impact of the theory of a conspiratorial élite, by permitting some discussion and debate within the élite itself and also within the framework of its Marxist assumptions.

But from the beginning centralism and discipline were the operative terms much more than democracy. To be sure, following the seizure of power in November 1917, debates at Party Congresses continued down to 1925. Yet, as early as 1921, at the Party Congress that passed the New Economic Policy, Lenin got up to say that he regarded the recent discussions of this topic as an absolutely impermissible luxury. He persuaded the Congress to outlaw Party fractions in the future. A secret clause in the Party's decree, later revealed by Stalin, provided for expulsion of a member of the Central Committee who violated the new rules against such behaviour.[11] Not long afterwards, in the spring of 1922, Lenin again used his authority to give legal sanction to the use of revolutionary terror on a permanent basis.[12]

Thus Lenin prepared the way for Stalin's silencing of public debates within the Party and his terrorist rule over Soviet society. It is necess-

ary to stress this point because well-intentioned critics of Stalin have
tried to glorify Lenin as a figure of contrast. About Stalin himself I will
say no more than a few words at this point. His opponents accused him
of packing Party Congresses with his own supporters and using the
secret police to intimidate his opponents. Whatever his methods were,
they worked. After the Fourteenth Party Congress, held in December,
1925, public attacks on the persons and policies of the Party leadership
ceased.[13] Thus, the pressure of chronic emergency combined with the
will of leaders, firmly committed to the concept of a revolutionary élite,
to tame the power of the rank and file in the Bolshevik Party. The same
thing happened to the soviets, to the system of authority in the
factories, and to workers' discipline. Each of these we shall discuss
briefly. The subjection of the peasantry to socialist controls was one of
the most brutal transformations in human history and requires separate analysis.

The taming of the soviets, or more precisely their subordination to
the will of the top Party leadership, was a more complex and uneven
process than the taming of the Party itself. Originally the soviets sprang
up, as spontaneously as human social inventions ever do, in the
Revolution of 1905 and again in 1917. Prior to the Bolshevik takeover,
soviets were, theoretically at least, elective councils with a miscella-
neous set of functions and, as such reasonably authentic expressions of
the will of the revolutionized sector of the masses. Lenin, however, was
wary of the stability of their revolutionary mood as well as their
capacity—and that of the still tiny Bolshevik organization—to withstand a counter-revolutionary coup by the Provisional Government.
Hence, soon after his return to Russia in 1917, he set out to take
power independently of the soviets.[14] In the event, the actual seizure of
power went rather smoothly, encountering only minimal resistance.
But it took a civil war that lasted from the end of 1917 to the autumn of
1920 to consolidate this power.

In the meantime the Constitution of the Russian Socialist Feder-
ated Soviet Republic, adopted on 5 July 1918, had given expression to
what we can call the Bolshevik variant of populism. Its first paragraph
proclaimed that

Russia is a Republic of Soviets of Workers, Soldiers, and Peasant Deputies.
All power in the center and locally belongs to these Soviets.[15]

For a brief time, that may have been at best a pious wish in some
leading Bolshevik circles. But the circumstances of a civil war, with the

need for rapid decisions and centralized authority, were hardly favourable to putting such a wish into practice. For that matter it is highly unlikely that Lenin, or any other leading Bolshevik, ever wanted to give all power to the soviets. At any rate by the end of 1919 virtually all authority had become concentrated in the centre, and local soviets had ceased to have any importance.[16]

With the tightening of Party controls, on the other hand, new problems appeared that were to be a more or less permanent feature of the Soviet regime. If the Party retained an iron hand over the soviets and usurped their functions, there was the danger of apathy, lack of obedience and support at the grass roots, and even outright hostility. But the opposite policy of loosening Party controls threatened even worse dangers: elements hostile to the government might get themselves elected to the soviets and distort or sabotage Party policies from within.

The Party tried to resolve this dilemma by 'enlivening the soviets', that is, making their style of decision-making more democratic, and by holding new elections in the hope of infusing a more proletarian personnel.[17] These devices enjoyed no more than limited success. A decree of the Central Committee of 21 December 1930 on new elections to the soviets echoed many of the complaints issued after the 1926 elections. In 1930, however, the situation was different. The USSR was in the throes of what Stalin was to call the revolution from above. This revolution transformed Soviet society through collectivization in agriculture, planning, and forced-draft growth in industry. In these new circumstances the Party leaders found the soviets to be lagging badly.[18]

Glancing ahead somewhat at random one finds similar complaints about 'major shortcomings' in the work of the soviets voiced in a similar decree of 22 January 1957—almost four years after the death of Stalin.[19] There is a difference, nevertheless, in that the 1957 complaints are concerned mainly with consumers' problems, while the earlier Party strictures had to do with complaints about failure to promote production. Production problems came to the fore again after Brezhnev's death. In other words, the functions or tasks of the soviets changed in response to changes in the character of Soviet society and the strategy of its leaders.

What, then, are the functions of the soviets that change in this manner while the complaints remain nearly constant? Originally, the soviets seem to have been thought of as self-governing cells in a system of self-government, though I am unaware of any serious attempt to put such ideas into practice amid the flames of revolution and civil war. By the time the Party had gained control over the soviets, if not earlier, it is plain that the Party wanted to make them the enthusiastic executors of Party policy at the local level. They were also expected to be the Party's agents of supervision from below, over the bottom levels of the government bureaucracy, to prevent, for example, haughty and rude treatment of the population. However, since campaigns against various bureaucratic distortions usually start at the highest levels of the regime, it is doubtful that local soviets ever had much freedom of manœuvre in opening and closing the safety valves that control the currents of popular discontent. These safety valves have always remained securely in the hands of the Party and the police. The most important element in the situation appears to be that enthusiasm at the local level tends to wither from contact with apathy or even hostility among the general population. Moreover, many local soviet officials, including no doubt some Party members, feel that there is precious little they can do about the misfortune and miseries they see around them.

In this sense the repeated complaints by the Party leadership about local weaknesses and failures indicate a general failure of authority in the Soviet regime. The Party leadership has not been able to transmit downward into the society at large the kind of enthusiastic and intelligent support it wants. Nevertheless, it would be a serious error to overestimate the importance of this particular evidence. No modern government ever gets anything like the support it wants, a result of the spread of democratic ideas. Earlier governments often did not care much about popular support so long as there were no serious revolts. A modern totalitarian regime, on the other hand, seeks total support and total enthusiasm, so long as it is in charge of the enthusiasm. Hence signs of apathy and discontent can easily become exaggeratd when they are perceived through the eyes of a totalitarian regime. Finally, the Soviet regime has survived for well over three generations, with a substantial sector of the population alienated from this regime. During these years it has encountered severe internal crises and a devastating war. If the failure of authority is a serious malady in the body politic of the USSR, it must be a very slow-acting one and hardly a mortal illness.

The soviets are agents of authority and enthusiasm all over the USSR. We have now to concentrate briefly on a narrower field: authority in industry and discipline over the workers in the workers'

state. Once more I shall refer mainly to the earlier phases of the regime
to show the experiences and ideas that led to later practices.

Shortly before the Bolshevik Revolution, Lenin had claimed that
capitalism had so greatly simplified the functions of management in
modern society that any literate file-clerk could perform them at
workmen's wages. He was also in favour of planning and centralized
control. For these, too, capitalism had supposedly prepared the
ground. By the time of the Revolution, centralized control was very
much in the air because belligerents on both sides were resorting to it
heavily during the First World War.

On the other hand, when the Revolution came, the leaders had little
hesitation in setting notions of centralized control aside, at least for the
time being. Bolshevik power was shaky. They could hardly make a
proletarian revolution in the name of peace in order to install what
looked like wartime controls, at least not now. Instead, and at Lenin's
instance, in the famous decree on Workers' Control, the Bolsheviks
turned the factories over to the workers to run as best they could,
much as they turned over the land to the peasants to let them run that
as best they could.

At the time workers' control meant little more than an official
blessing for the workers' attempts to take control in other cities besides
the capital, a movement the Bolsheviks could hardly afford to discour-
age. General elections were to be held in each plant over a certain size
to determine who was to represent the workers and who was to manage
the plant. About 40 per cent of the factories in the area of Russia
controlled by the Bolsheviks were affected by the system of workers'
control. The workers proceeded to promote the interests of their own
factories with little or no regard to the interests of society at large or
the state. There was, as yet, no way to co-ordinate the production of
the various factories, to make sure that if a factory turned out screws of
a certain size and thread, there was some other unit in the economy
that needed these screws. The role of the state fell to that of paying
subsidies. Such a system could not and did not last long. By the
beginning of 1918 this experiment came to an end.[20]

In the spring of that year and in the course of a revealing general
review of the immediate tasks facing the new regime, Lenin made
some remarks on management and the discipline of the labour force
that were to enter the canon of Soviet theory on this topic. He wrote in
Pravda of 28 April 1918 that,

We must learn to combine the meeting democracy of the toiling masses—turbulent, surging, overflowing its banks like a spring flood—with *iron* discipline while at work, with *unquestioning obedience* to the will of a single person, the Soviet manager, while at work.[21]

To sustain this turbulent enthusiasm and combine it with strict subjection to authority would be a most difficult task indeed. By the time Stalinism was well established, say about 1930, the emphasis came to be on discipline while enthusiasm had become a public-relations product to be expressed at carefully staged gatherings in support of official objectives.

In the early years of power the Bolsheviks were still searching for viable forms of management compatible with a fledgling socialist society. By about 1919 the prevailing practice was collegial management. Boards were set up composed of two-thirds workers and one-third engineers or technicians approved by the trade unions. Though the role of technical skill was now recognized, a great deal of confusion remained. During 1919 and 1920 there was much discussion of the problems of democratic management in high Party circles. Tomsky, a trade-union leader and member of the Workers' Opposition argued that collegial management was the only method capable of achieving broad mass participation in the management of industry. Lenin's reply was vitriolic.

You cannot escape . . . by declaring that corporate management is a school of government . . . You cannot stay forever in the preparatory class of a school . . . We are now grown up, and we shall be beaten and beaten again in every field if we behave like school children.

For Lenin there was only one answer: *yedinonachaliye*, i.e., one-man management, or more loosely expressed, individual responsibility and authority. That had been the direction in which industrial practice had begun to move anyway. By 1920 eighty-five per cent of the enterprises in the new regime were controlled by individual managers, though their powers were weak.[22] The Ninth Party Congress, held from 29 March to 5 April 1920, gave the *coup de grâce* to the principle of collegiality by declaring that, 'collegiality, however much a place it has in the process of reaching a judgement or a decision, must unconditionally give way to one-man management in the process of execution'.[23]

The theory and practice of one-man management did not shake down into a moderately settled form until after the Stalinist revolution from above. Shortly before Stalin's death the second edition of the

Great Soviet Encyclopaedia published a definition of one-man management that put a heavy stress on the aspects of undivided authority and clear responsibility. It described one-man management as

... the basic method of leadership in a socialist economy and government apparatus, consisting in the fact that the person in authority bears personal responsibility toward the government for the work of the enterprise or establishment entrusted to him and is invested with the complete power necessary for the successful realization of leadership over that enterprise or establishment.[24]

Taken by itself there is nothing in this definition that would distinguish Soviet management from its American counterpart.

From this authoritative description one could gain the mistaken impression that one-man management had completely replaced collegiality as a principle of authority in industry. In my judgement that would be a serious error. Looking over the evidence from refugee accounts and the press about what industrial managers actually did, one can see very quickly that management retained strong collegial elements. Only the democratic and populist aspects have disappeared from collegiality. Workers played no role in industrial management. But the manager or director, as he was usually called, had to manœuvre and bargain with several officials to keep production going. Any one of them could mount an effective challenge to the director. One was the secretary of the Party organization in the factory or plant. Another was the chief of the 'special section' or secret police unit. By far the weakest of the three with outside connections was the head of the trade-union committee. Inside the plant or factory were the chief engineer, the head of the department of technical control (roughly similar to our 'quality control' whose job is to make sure that the quality is not one bit better than necessary so as to avoid wasting materials), and finally the chief bookkeeper.[25] The relationship among this cumbersome set of officials exemplifies what I have elsewhere called the vested interest in confusion, the need to keep subordinates unsure of themselves in order to maintain control from on high. Simultaneously, it probably reflects the need to put something in the place of the discipline of the market over the processes of production. Caution, however, is necessary on this score. In our oligopolist economy the discipline of the market works slowly and imperfectly, leaving in 'normal' times plenty of room for maladministration and neglect of the customer's interest.

What happened to the workers and industrial discipline with the advent of socialism? By Stalin's time official doctrine had come to hold that socialist labour discipline had nothing to do with the cruel and exploitative discipline of capitalist society. Instead, under socialism there is social ownership of the means of production, and therefore the workers allegedly do their jobs conscientiously, indeed with pride and enthusiasm.[26] To the best of my knowledge and belief such claims are pure but necessary nonsense. In the early days of the new regime Lenin made some remarks along these lines, duly quoted in the exposition of canonical doctrine that I have just summarized. If one looks up these remarks in their original context, one sees that Lenin was not so much interested in conceptions of socialist discipline as in getting workers to work at all.

A few weeks after the seizure of power he pointed out that the Party would have to fight the workers' ' . . . habit of shirking burdens, of trying to get as much as possible out of the *bourgeoisie*'. Newcomers who entered factory life during the war, were, he complained, especially bad: ' . . . they want to treat the *people's* factory, the factory that has come into the possession of the people, in the old way, with the sole end in view of "making" as much as possible and clearing out'.[27] Lenin blamed these defects on the Russian experience of capitalism and the survival of petty-bourgeois individualism among the workers. There is considerable merit to such an explanation when added to the general confusion of the times. Nevertheless, it is significant that so many workers, at least in Lenin's eyes, showed such a reluctance to work hard on behalf of 'their' government at a time of high revolutionary enthusiasm. To be sure, pockets of enthusiasm did appear later in the form of the well-known Saturday workers or free evening and holiday workers. But these remained merely pockets.

The underlying issue likewise remained. As Lenin's remarks show, from the very beginning the Party leadership was very reluctant to perceive or state openly that under socialism too there would be a built-in conflict of interests between management and workers. For a time the existence of such a conflict could be explained away with phrases about the survival of capitalist traits. As this explanation became less plausible with the passing of time and the Bolshevik variant of socialism became more firmly established, the simple ritual denial of a conflict of interests became more insistent.

To return to the early phase of the new regime, some sort of discipline had to be re-established in industry no matter what political label it bore. The issue was a burning one for the Party, and the source of organized opposition movements within the Party from 1918 through part of 1921. From these debates I will select a few remarks by Trotsky because of the way they foreshadowed later developments under Stalin.

As an outstanding military leader during the Civil War it is hardly surprising that Trotsky advocated a military solution to the problems created by the workers. On 9 April 1920, he announced to the Third Congress of Trade Unions that the unions did not have the task of fighting against the government in the interests of labour. Instead, they ought to co-operate with the government in the task of constructing a socialist economy. Attacking the Mensheviks for spreading the idea that compulsory labour was inefficient he asserted,

If that is true, then the entire socialist economy is destined to crash, for there can be no other road to socialism except the compulsory distribution of the entire labour force of the country by the central economic authority, which will distribute this force according to the needs of an over-all government economic plan.

The militarization of labour was necessary, he claimed, under which the unions should help in allocating workers to their posts. To the Mensheviks such proposals looked like Egyptian slavery. Trotsky replied that Egyptian peasants did not decide through their soviets to build the pyramids.[28]

Anyone with a fondness for historical irony could claim that Trotsky was a premature Stalinist because Stalin eventually adopted so many of Trotsky's proposed policies. With the onset of large-scale industrialization in 1929 and 1930 the workers were called upon to make heavy sacrifices. The Party compelled them to give up the limited degree of independent representation of their interests by the unions that Lenin had insisted upon against Trotsky, and that was tolerated in the early twenties under the New Economic Policy. In the spring of 1930 almost the entire leadership of the All-Union Council of Trade Unions was removed and replaced by men willing to support Stalin's programmes of greatly increasing labour productivity. There was hardly any pretence that the Party Central Committee's action was in accord with Soviet conceptions of democracy. One of Stalin's top administrators, Lazar Kaganovich, dismissed such objections with remarks that reveal a great deal about current Soviet conceptions of authority:

One might say that this is a violation of proletarian democracy, but, comrades, it has long been known that for us Bolsheviks democracy is not a fetish; for us, proletarian democracy is a means for arming the working class for the better execution of its socialist tasks.[29]

This is not the place to discuss the further development of controls over labour, except to point out that they were always mitigated by the existence of a de facto free market for labour, which was in turn the result of a severe shortage of manpower. Factory managers who needed workers badly were disinclined to check closely whether a worker had authorization to leave his previous job.

4   *The Stalinist revolution from above*

Instead, let us turn now to the Stalinist revolution from above as necessary background for the Stalinist terror, certainly a key aspect of authority in the Soviet system. By high-speed industrialization, planning, and the collectivization of agriculture, the revolution from above had a powerful impact on the lives of just about every Soviet citizen and transformed Russian society from top to bottom. All this happened between 1929 and 1934. Further changes followed after 1934 as the Soviet Union became one of the world's great industrial and military powers. But these changes were more of the same. The basic pattern had been set during those years. I cannot think of any deliberate social transformation at any time in human history that was so swift and so thorough. Indeed, transformation is a euphemism. In the short run the revolution from above was a man-made disaster. In the longer run it was a success in so far as the leaders who carried it out—except for those executed at Stalin's orders—remained in control and, with the help of the Allies, defeated Nazi Germany. Even the success has its ambiguities. The wounds Stalin inflicted on Soviet society very likely contributed to the initial German victories in the invasion of Russia that began in June 1941.

To understand why the revolution from above occurred it is necessary to look briefly at the situation in the late 1920s. As early as 1926 the Russian economy had for the most part recovered to the level attained just before the First World War. But the production of pig iron and steel—distinguishing features of an industrial economy—still lagged well below the levels reached in 1913.[30] Factory production, the 'commanding heights' of the economy, remained overwhelmingly in the hands of the state.[31] In the sense, then, of a general economic recovery with the Bolsheviks still in charge, the New Economic Policy of freedom to trade and reduced pressure on the peasants looked like a success. On the other hand, the success also looked like opening the door to capitalism, an idea which troubled some Bolshevik leaders. There are reasons for thinking this threat was more imaginary than real, even if it played a part in the decision to impose socialism from above. As long as the Party kept control of big industry, it had the means to control the flow of essential supplies to the rest of the economy. There were ways, in other words, to keep petty capitalism under control, if that is what the Bolsheviks wanted. But they wanted a great deal more.

In addition to the general problem of socialist economic recovery under capitalist auspices there were two more specific problems facing the Soviet leaders. After 1923 the government continued to pursue a policy of price cuts for goods produced by state trusts. Since there were not enough goods to meet demand at lowered prices, the government extended price control over an ever wider portion of state industry, state and co-operative trade. The predictable result was a 'goods famine', that is, there was little or nothing to be had in the market at official prices. Private trade that was still permitted took on the characteristics of speculation since it was profitable to buy state-produced goods for resale. Thus one effect was to transfer resources to the private sector. Another effect was to limit the supply of goods available to the peasants, especially those in villages far from towns, since the towns swallowed up first what goods were available at low prices. Peasants had to pay more if they got anything at all.

Persistence in holding prices below the market value of goods is partly traceable to Bolshevik hostility to market forces. It was also partly due to the severe internal rivalries among Party leaders. The basic dilemma was that, in order to correct the situation, the Party would have to give greater freedom to market forces or else destroy the market and its manifestations.[32]

The peasants constituted the second major problem. By the middle and late 1920s the effect of the Bolshevik Revolution turned out to be what would now be called a variety of land reform. The holdings of landlords and larger peasants disappeared. Millions of landless labourers and ex-peasants, who had returned from town in the days of war communism, acquired land. The number of family holdings rose from about 18 million in 1917 to 25 million in 1927.[33] As is usually the case with land reform, the change diminished the surplus of food available to feed the towns because this surplus came in large measure from the larger holdings. Also, as the poorer peasants became less

poor, they ate more, reducing further the amount of food available for
the urban dwellers. The shortage of marketed produce remained
chronic under the NEP. The shortages were intensified by the low
productivity and the technical and social backwardness of Russian
agriculture. The NEP was the golden age of the Russian village
community—where all decisions in the agricultural cycle were subject
to collective control. The three-field system, ownership by strips, and
dwarf holdings were widespread. As late as 1928 about one household
in five still used a wooden plough, and half the grain harvest was
reaped by sickle or scythe.[34]

Drastic changes would have to take place in agriculture if Russia was
going to modernize and feed its towns, no matter what the political
beliefs of the modernizers were. In reaching the pre-war level of
output, economic recovery had gone about as far as it could. New
capital investment would be needed and more food to feed the towns.
Above I suggested that these and the other problems of the day were
soluble within the framework of the NEP and continued Bolshevik
control of the commanding heights of the economy. But there were
certainly political risks to a slow and steady industrialization in the
manner of the NEP. The state would be dependent for food on the
output of well-to-do peasant proprietors with no love for the Bolsheviks. There would also be a growth of petty capitalism in the towns.
Sooner or later the Bolsheviks, whose support among the industrial
workers was still precarious, could find themselves politically
swamped. They might have to abdicate the goal of socialism or
postpone its realization to an indefinite future. The international
situation of alleged capitalist encirclement would not, it seemed, permit this kind of indefinite delay. Thus fears for political survival were
inextricably mingled with the goal that made survival worthwhile and
necessary. Without the goal the concrete problems would have
appeared much more manageable.[35]

Important as the commitment to socialism was, by itself that was not
the most important element. Among many Bolsheviks there was a
commitment to the means of getting there: speedy industrial growth
under centralized control, which of course meant Bolshevik control. It
was the speed that carried with it the commitment to coercion, though
it is highly unlikely that any Bolshevik leader, even Stalin, realized the
amount of coercion that would take place. Perhaps the commitment to
a furious tempo of industrialization was a matter of temperament
rather than of carefully thought out strategy. Be that as it may, such a

commitment was characteristic of Bolshevik revolutionary traditions. These had always emphasized the role of a committed élite in bringing about revolutionary changes against apparently overwhelming odds.

Widespread coercion began in agriculture even before the formal adoption of the first Five Year Plan. Toward the end of December 1927 state procurements of grain began to falter. Peasants were waiting for a rise in official grain prices, for which the prospects seemed reasonably good. By January of 1928 the state had managed to buy less than three-quarters of the amount purchased the previous year. Shortages were becoming acute, indeed threatening. At this juncture Stalin took off for the Urals and West Siberia, where the harvest had been reasonably good, with a task force of officials and police. They closed free markets, threw out private traders, ordered peasants to deliver grain, and punished them as criminals if they failed to do so. Stalin denounced laggard officials who were reluctant to seize grain from the better-off peasants (or *kulaks*) by invoking a hitherto unused article of the criminal code against speculation. He also used extreme language to Party officials slow to comprehend that their basic attitude of caution toward the peasantry must change. Stalin's actions became known as the 'Urals–Siberian method' and foreshadowed collectivization and the liquidation of the kulaks as a class. Thus, as Professor Nove points out, the Urals–Siberian method constitutes a great turning-point in Russian history.[36]

The first Five Year Plan was announced in May 1929. In December of that year Stalin asserted and justified the liquidation of the kulaks as a class, a process that had in fact begun in some localities before he spoke.[37] Other peasants were to lose their land and animals, as under compulsion they pooled their possessions to join a collective farm. Rather than give up their stock many peasants slaughtered them, leaving Russia with a chronic shortage of meat that persists to this day. Collectivization was carried through amidst tremendous confusion and brutality, with wide variations in its impact from one place to another. There were also variations in the policy of the central authority, including a major but temporary retreat by Stalin. I cannot discuss these aspects here. It is enough to emphasize the chaotic and arbitrary character of authority in relation to the overwhelming mass of the population at this time. A declaration of the Party's agitation and propaganda department in January 1930 gives some idea of the situation: 'If in some matters you commit excesses and you are arrested, remember that you have been arrested for your revolutionary deeds.'[38]

It is possible to form no more than a very rough notion of the social costs of this upheaval. The total number of kulaks was in the order of four and a half million people. Just what liquidation meant for these people is unclear. Many probably died while others were deported or exiled to remote areas of Russia.[39] In 1933 the combination of terror, disorganization, and the state's high rate of procurements—even though these had been reduced well below the impossible figure set in the plan—produced a famine. How many died we do not know. But Professor Nove calculates on the basis of census data that some ten million people 'demographically' disappeared between 1932 and 1939.[40] In other words, at the previous rate of increase, the population in 1939 would have been some ten million more than it actually was. This figure reflects in part a fall in the birth rate due to harsh conditions of life in both urban and rural areas. Furthermore, it includes the victims of the Great Terror, which appears to have been at its height around 1936. Therefore, the number of deaths due to the collectivization drive must have been well under ten million.

Though the manipulation of such grisly and not very reliable statistics is an unavoidable part of any effort to get at the truth, I will confess to some uneasiness in so doing. The process of counting, adding, and subtracting, necessarily disregards human differences and obliterates individual human tragedies. All of us who work with such figures have to remember that behind each digit there stands that many mortal sorrows.

What did Stalin and his associates get out of collectivization? At one time many scholars held that the collectivization of agriculture was a key aspect of the primitive socialist accummulation of capital. By this they meant that the new socialist state extracted from agriculture by force and fraud a substantial portion of the resources that went into the building of factories for the great drive toward industrialization. In the late 1960s and early 1970s this thesis underwent sceptical scrutiny. The most severe blow to it came in 1974 when James R. Millar published an interpretative review of two works by a Soviet economic historian, A. A. Barsov, who drew upon a great deal of previously inaccessible archival data in an attempt to measure directly the net material contribution of agriculture to industrialization. According to this evidence, agriculture was actually a net recipient of material resources just before the First Five Year Plan and during it. State investments in the state farm system (*sovkhozy*) and in the machine tractor system to service the collective farms (*kolkhozy*) appear to have been large enough to give agriculture a net inflow of funds. Another factor was the rise in prices for those goods which the peasants were permitted to sell in the open market.[41] There are grounds for great scepticism about this last point. To be sure, prices for privately traded agricultural commodities went through the roof, rising in 1932 to some thirty times the level of 1928. But that is liable to be merely a sign that there was practically nothing to sell.[42] Without knowing how many collective farmers could profit from such a windfall, and by how much each could profit in the course of a year, we do not really know anything. Reservations are also in order about the argument as a whole because it is precisely what a loyal Soviet citizen would want to prove. Any Stalinist would be delighted to learn that Stalin did not really squeeze the life out of the peasants in order to build socialism but instead tried to give agriculture technical assistance for the sake of modernization. On balance, nevertheless, there appears to be enough solid factual evidence now to require that we discard any theory of primitive socialist accumulation based on extracting resources from agriculture.

There is no doubt, on the other hand, that Stalin did achieve one central objective: an increase in state grain collections. In 1928, the last year before collectivization, state grain procurements were only 10.8 million tons. By 1930 they were already up to 22.1 million tons and remained in this vicinity through 1933, except for a fall-back to 18.5 tons in 1932, a year in which Stalin decided to relax procurements somewhat.[43] But even this victory may have come about accidentally and certainly at a very heavy price, with long lasting effects on food production in the USSR. The entire increase in grain procurements is, according to good authority, more than explained by the drop in fodder requirements caused by the peasants' wholesale destruction of livestock herds at the onset of collectivization.[44] In addition to breaking the peasants' economic stranglehold on food supplies for the cities, collectivization destroyed the prospect for local peasant uprisings or more peaceful forms of concerted political action. At one stroke Stalin destroyed the muzhik as the real autocrat of all Russia (a description common before the revolution). Finally, it seems likely that many peasants found they could not make ends meet in the country-side and migrated to the towns, increasing thereby the pool of labour needed for the industrial spurt.

The general achievements of the revolution from above were indeed striking. Between 1927–8 and 1932 the Soviet Union laid the foundations for a mighty industrial state under centralized planning, which meant, in effect, control by the top leadership of the Party. Gross industrial production, measured in hundred millions of 1926-7 rubles, rose from 18.3 in 1927-8 to 43.3 in 1932.[45] Though such figures conceal shortfalls in specific industrial sectors—steel production was obviously disappointing—and give little indication of the quality of goods turned out, there is hardly any reason to doubt that, in terms of the Stalinists' overall political objectives, this plan and those that succeeded it during Stalin's lifetime were a success.

The costs of this use of political authority to make the Soviet version of a Great Leap Forward were painful. The most painful ones fell upon the peasants. In the cities, real wages appear to have dropped. Housing was extremely scarce. Rationing and shortages were widespread. All in all, according to Professor Nove, the year 1933 seems to have marked 'the culmination of the most precipitous decline in living standards known in human history'.[46]

Reactions to the hardships, sacrifices, and confused turmoil that were part of the pursuit of so mighty a goal, were diverse and contradictory. No doubt there was much grumbling to the effect that we can't eat statistics. But grumbling could be dangerous and land the discontented in a distant labour camp. At the other end of the scale were the genuine enthusiasm and faith in the future displayed by many thousands of technicians and workers, especially young people. Among others slightly higher in the scale there was a recrudescence of extreme leftism. These were people who regarded considerations of cost as a relic of bourgeois ideology and who idealized communal living, which was in fact a consequence of overcrowding.[47] This form of radicalism, which was also very prominent immediately after the Bolshevik Revolution, seems to flourish best in the times of chaos and shortages that are especially hard on ordinary people.

On the other hand, the drift of official policy was against any extreme leftism. Stalin dumped overboard the egalitarian elements in Marxism. On 23 June 1931, in a speech to a conference of business executives, he attacked sharply the 'Leftist' practice of wage equalization that was wiping out the difference between skilled and unskilled labour. He wanted to end the heavy turnover of labour, keeping a cadre of skilled workers in each factory. Skilled and unskilled workers were to be encouraged to stop floating from factory to factory by improving the supply of products, housing, and other material and cultural conditions of life.[48] At this time too there began to flourish, amid the shortages, a system of special privileges for selected categories of workers and especially for officials. The privileges consisted of such things as access to 'closed' stores carrying otherwise unobtainable foods and other goods, allocations of tolerable housing or even a good apartment, or a permit to buy a good suit. Under conditions of universal scarcity money could do little. But authority could reward its own with small and not so small favours.[49] Such practices, as Professor Nove points out, readily lent themselves to abuse. Here we can see the origin of the corruption that, according to many observers, permeates so much of the Soviet bureaucracy today. Here, too, in the frayed tempers that afflicted so many, we can see the source of the rudeness and arrogance that mars so much of official behaviour toward ordinary citizens, especially in their role as consumers.

5 *The terror, its causes and consequences*

The deep wounds inflicted on Soviet society by collectivization and industrialization were an important cause of the Great Terror that followed shortly afterward. But the terror was not, in my judgement, an inevitable consequence of these wounds. Conceivably, a different type of leadership might have combined a policy of healing and reconciliation with a strictly limited use of punitive weapons to achieve similar or even better results.

Before discussing the causes it is necessary to explain briefly, yet concretely, the meaning of terror in the specific context of Soviet society. I shall use the term very broadly to refer to a set of five punitive measures, listed in order of increasing severity. The justification for lumping all five together is that any one of them was frightening and could, especially in the atmosphere of the Great Terror, lead to other and more severe measures. The first and least severe measure was the ordinary purge, used mainly in the Party, but also from time to time in any set of administrative offices. A purged Party member lost his or her membership in the Party. Theoretically such a person would not lose his or her job, though this often happened. Being purged from an administrative post could mean, for a non-Party person, transfer to a less responsible post or to unemployment. The second and third measures were arrest and confinement to an ordinary prison. The fourth measure, transfer to a labour camp, might follow. Or the fifth alternative, execution, might follow imprisonment. There were also executions in the camps.

Though terror existed from just about the beginning of the Bolshevik regime (a decree of 5 September 1918 authorized the establishment of concentration camps)[50] its most intense form did not appear until 1936–8, the years of the Great Purge. At first glance the delay is puzzling. By that time the Soviet system had taken its basic form. Anti-Bolshevik enemies were thoroughly crushed. Within the Party Stalin seemed victorious and his policies vindicated. According to general theories of revolution one would expect the maximum of terror to occur shortly after the revolutionaries took power. Then the revolutionaries could be expected to destroy their opponents and settle accounts with the old regime in order to prepare the way for a new social order. Conceivably, one could make the facts fit this theory by expanding the definition of terror to include the White casualties in the Civil War. Yet even granting this point would not help to explain the Great Terror that seemed to surge out of nowhere almost a generation later.

We will come back to the timing later after discussing factors that made the terror possible though not necessarily inevitable. One set of factors was the body of habits and traditions concerning the treatment of political opponents that grew up under Lenin's guidance in the Bolshevik Party. It was Lenin who conferred legitimacy on the use of terror and refused to set any limits on its application. So far as I am aware Lenin encountered no serious opposition to his proposals. It was Lenin too who set an example of verbal savagery toward political opponents, especially those expressing views close to his own. This practice is almost certainly no invention by Lenin; a very similar polemical style may be found in Marx.[51] It is also necessary to point out that with regard to Party comrades Lenin never took the step from verbal abuse to physical liquidation. It was left to Stalin to break this taboo. If Robert Conquest is correct, Stalin had a great deal of difficulty in persuading the top Party leadership to endorse this step.[52]

One final aspect of the general situation prior to the drive for collectivization and industrialization deserves mention here because it must have influenced policy-making at the highest levels. Early in 1921, high Party leaders realized that they had lost the support of the industrial workers amid the sacrifices of the Civil War and War Communism. Radek said so openly in an address to War College cadets, adding characteristically that the Party must not yield to this reactionary sense of exhaustion but impose its will to victory on its dispirited followers.[53] Equally characteristically for that historical period, the Party did in fact yield some weeks later and introduced the

New Economic Policy. Nevertheless, this episode reveals the Party's conception of itself as a beleaguered revolutionary élite, not an élite with powerful support from the masses. Secondly, it expresses a clear willingness to impose the Party's will on the masses if the latter become disenchanted. From there it is not a very long step to reorganizing society in order to control the masses. That of course happened in 1929–30. But not all the consequences were foreseen or foreseeable.

Another set of causes may be found in the legacy of the drive toward high-speed industrialization and collectivization, together with the Party disputes that preceded this drive. As everyone knows, in the course of coming to these major decisions, Stalin drove his opponents out of the Party, changing his policies according to his perception of the tactical needs of the moment.

As the drive gathered speed, some of his right-wing opponents were thoroughly frightened at the prospect of Stalin leading the Party and the country to chaos and catastrophe if he failed, to a police state if he succeeded. (On the latter score they were of course correct, though it is not easy to see what else could be expected.) Between 1930 and 1933 there were three organized opposition movements in the Party directed against Stalin. In 1934 at the Seventeenth Party Congress there was evidently some talk behind the scenes of replacing Stalin with S. M. Kirov and curbing the terror that had already begun to grow.[54] Presumably all of these leading elements in the Party had at least some supporters in the rank and file. Furthermore, the tense situation in the country as a whole must have generated somewhat similar sentiments among a substantial number of ordinary people inside and outside the Party. Foreign Communists who visited the USSR in the early thirties and became disillusioned by what they encountered found themselves almost automatically put in touch with an organized grass-roots opposition within the Soviet Party.[55] Outside the Party too, the revolution from above had created many and varied reasons for resentment and suspicion. Many a city dweller must have had rural relatives or acquaintances who were perceived as the victims of brutal injustice. For workers in the towns discipline had become harsh and real wages had fallen, while administrators faced heavy penalties if they failed in impossible tasks. Despite the existence of indubitable enthusiasm, there are many indications of hostility and doubt.

All such sentiments Stalin chose to excise surgically from the body politic in the way that a skilled ship's carpenter removes tainted timbers from a wooden vessel. To me the Great Terror remains inexplicable without the decisive cause that was Stalin's character. He was highly vindictive and suspicious almost to the point of paranoia. Yet he was no quasi-religious fanatic. Two influences permeate his writings and formal speeches: the seminary and Leninized Marxism. The latter provided some intellectual categories and simple rules for manipulating them, as in class analysis. None of his thought could ever be seen as profound or elevating. An English wit remarked many years ago that Stalin frequently suffered from vertigo on the higher Hegelian trapezes. Yet neither his intellectual qualities nor lack of them seem to have been decisive in bringing on the terror. The causes lay deeper in his character in the form of sheer vindictive suspiciousness.

To summarize the factors behind an admittedly puzzling sequence of events I suggest that the destructive Bolshevik attitude toward opposition, an awareness of their position as a revolutionary élite with hardly any mass following, fear and distrust of Stalin's Great Leap Forward in high Party circles, together with antagonisms and resentments it had created among the general population, all made the Great Terror possible and perhaps even likely. But it was Stalin's vindictive suspiciousness that made it happen, and made it happen when it did. Only when he had gained supreme power could he unleash the terror. For Stalin the terror was vengeance and social prophylaxis, a device to ensure that his brand of socialism would not be challenged from within.

Once the Soviet terror had begun it expanded rapidly. Part of this expansion was the result of pure bureaucratic momentum. The secret police had a job to do and wanted to make it as big and important as possible. They created a huge network of informers who had to prove their vigilance against spies, wreckers, and subversive elements. Rank and file Party members and even ordinary citizens also had to demonstrate vigilance, or so they were led to think. In fact vigilance was no guarantee of security. Every arrest created a nest of further suspects because relatives and friends of the victims were by and large correctly suspected of turning against the government. Thus one of the consequences of the terror was to reduce sharply the legitimacy of the regime, to replace legitimate authority with naked power and widespread fear.

The primary effect of the terror was to destroy those Party leaders and their followers who might become rivals to Stalin or oppose his policies. We get some sense of the range of this slaughter by noting the fate of the 1,966 delegates to the Seventeenth Party Congress that met in January 1934 to celebrate Stalin's victory in the drive toward industrialization and collectivization. Ironically Stalin said to this Congress that there were no more anti-Leninist groupings and, there-fore, 'nothing to prove and, it seems nobody to beat'. In the next few years 1,108 of the 1,966 delegates who listened to Stalin were shot.[56] A total of thirty-three men became members of the Politburo between 1919 and 1938. Under Stalin this became an extremely dangerous occupation. Sixteen of these men were shot or assassinated, and one committed suicide. All of these deaths are traceable to Stalin, except possibly that of S. M. Kirov. Conquest and others, however, have argued that Stalin plotted his death too.[57] The casualties in the Politburo and among the delegates to the Seventeenth Party Congress constitute no more than a partial list of those in the Party as a whole. The impact of the terror does appear to have been especially severe on the Party's higher ranks. But it was by no means limited to them.

Another major effect—or should we say purpose?—was to destroy the leadership of any social formation, such as the army or the police, that might be able to wall itself off from pressures affecting the rest of Soviet society and thereby escape the control of the Stalinist leadership or even form a nucleus for opposition to it. If anything, the terrorist purge struck more heavily at the military than the Party. Three of the five Marshals were victims; fourteen of the sixteen Army Com-manders, Classes I and II; all of the eight Admirals, Classes I and II; and so on in roughly similar proportions, down to 221 of the 397 Brigade Commanders. Below the upper echelons around half of the officer corps, some 35,000 in all, were shot or imprisoned.[58] In 1957 the second edition of the *Great Soviet Encyclopaedia* acknowledged that the 'illegal repressions of 1936–1939', carried out by 'mortal enemies of the people, Yagoda, Ezhov, and Beriya', all heads of the secret police and all in due course executed, who had 'insinuated themselves into the confidence of Stalin, . . . led to a well-known weakening of the military forces' at the outbreak of the war.[59] About the secret police we know very little more than the execution of its leaders. The top job seems to have been the most dangerous post of all in the whole Soviet system, and understandably so in the light of its awesome power. But the lightning did not strike there alone. The numerous tales among refugees about secret police officials turning up as their companions in jail suggest that there were purges in the lower ranks as well. Obviously the dictator would have to keep the secret police off-balance lest it turn against him.

There was a time when students of the Soviet Union thought that the terror affected mainly the upper ranks of the Soviet order and spared the general population. Evidence that became available shortly after the Second World War, in the form of Soviet classified documents captured by the Germans and numerous accounts by refugees, made it necessary to discard this opinion completely. On the basis of this evidence I was able to form the very rough guess that among the ordinary population the threat of arrest faced as many as one man in five at some point in their lives.[60]

The main social consequence of the terror among the general population was to penetrate and destroy the little cells based on friendship and co-operation that offered a limited degree of protection against the rigours of a totalitarian regime and opportunities to evade its orders. In other words, the population was to a high degree atomized. A great many individuals felt alone and defenceless. As numerous refugees remarked, there was nobody whom one could trust, not even close friends or family members. The situation put a premium on hypocrisy since the only recipe for safety—and a far from dependable recipe at that—was to mouth as convincingly as possible the approved attitudes of the day.

From Stalin's standpoint of wanting to control the population and suppress overt dissent, this destruction of the basic cells in the social order had some very positive features (though I doubt very much that Stalin thought about it in these terms.) From the standpoint of Soviet society as a whole the policy had some very negative features. Cells of evasion were, and are very often, at the same time co-operative units that keep the system going. A friendship group in a factory administration may have pull with someone in a ministry that enables the factory to get supplies without which work would come to a stop. Lower down the hierarchy, a worker in one of the factory's shops may have a friend in the stock-room who can give him a part without authorization. Otherwise the shop might have to cease operations. Higher up, the man in the ministry who got supplies for the factory will have to find someone in another ministry to replace these supplies. All this semi-legal activity works through personal connections. There are professionals who do nothing else but make these arrangements. It is easy to see how these semi-legal activities would provide a field-day for the secret police and their informers, and how much confusion and damage their destruction would cause. This, however, is only one form of necessary co-operation among the human beings that make up any complex or civilized society. It takes no great leap of the sociological imagination to see that the destruction of all these co-operative cells would destroy the society. Stalin either would not or could not go that far.

Because the Soviet Union continued to industrialize rapidly under the system of widespread terror, I once thought, along with other students of Soviet affairs that the terror must have contributed to this success.[61] Supposedly, the diffuse anxiety produced by the terror led people to put more effort into their work and make sure that their work was both accurate and satisfactory. That may well have been the case with a substantial scattering of individuals. But I have come to doubt that this reaction to fear made any large contribution to socialist construction. Instead, this type of argument may reflect the sociologist's tendency to find some contribution to the social order in just about any existing practice.

On general grounds I would now suggest that the contribution of the terror to socialist construction was on balance negative. One widespread reaction to fright is sheer paralysis and confusion. At the very least there is an avoidance of responsibility and the making of decisions. Neither paralysis nor the avoidance of responsibility could have served the purposes of the regime. Another reaction to danger that takes more time to develop is simply to become used to it to the point of ignoring it. So long as nothing happens one hopes or even believes that one will not be arrested. In the meantime the individual is likely to seek solace and security in the familiar round of daily routines. Bursts of energy or enthusiasm are something to avoid because they destroy the security of routine and make one conspicuous. That response, too, is hardly a useful one from the dictator's standpoint.

Though the weight of the terror is thought to have decreased somewhat after 1938, it never stopped as long as Stalin lived. With the outbreak of the war in 1941 there was a marked increase in the activity of the police.[62] Toward the end of Stalin's life the publicity given to the so-called 'doctors' plot' gave every sign of building up to another blood bath. Only his death on 5 March 1953 cut short this prospect. On 3 April 1953 *Pravda* and *Izvestia* announced that the arrest of the doctors had no lawful basis. *Pravda* carried further details on 6 April 1953, accusing a former Minister of State Security of political blindness. These dramatic events were part of a public campaign on behalf of a 'new legality', a campaign through which Stalin's successors sought to secure their position. According to their assessment it was necessary to reduce the terror sharply. This they appear to have done.

Just before the Second World War there were in the order of 3.5 million able-bodied workers in the camps.[63] Conquest asserts that in the 1960s there were about one million inmates.[64] I have not been able to find any more up-to-date figures. The number may well have dropped further, as other methods for coping with dissent, such as psychiatric hospitalization, have come along. Be that as it may, it is obvious that the threat of repression against political 'error' still lurks not very far in the background. On these grounds it remains appropriate to call the Soviet Union a police state, even if one with considerably reduced terror.

6 Inequalities in the age of Brezhnev

In addition to the reduction in terror, post-Stalinist Russia has displayed at least three trends that require brief mention as a background for some concluding observations on inequalities in contemporary Soviet society. One is a tendency toward stagnation or low rates of growth in Soviet industry. The second is a shift in the position of Soviet agriculture. From being an object of exploitation in the early thirties—even if there was less exploitation than Western authorities once believed—agriculture has become an object of government subsidies and a heavy drag on the government's budget.[65] This change appears to be part of a policy of raising the incomes of those at the bottom of the social heap, which began to be noticeable in the 1960s.[66] As such it constitutes a limited reversal of Stalin's anti-egalitarian policies announced in 1931 and carried on during his lifetime. On the other hand, there has been another trend that is hardly egalitarian and which is also characteristic of advanced capitalist societies: a marked increase in the size and privileges of the professional stratum.

As everyone knows by now, the Soviet Union is a highly stratified society. In terms of income and social esteem there is as great a social distance between a high political official and an unskilled farm labourer in the Soviet Union as there is between a justice of the Supreme Court and a ditch digger in the United States. There are, on the other hand, some important differences between the systems of inequality in these two countries. In the absence of private property in the means of production, a member of the Soviet élite is completely dependent on official position for access to the material goods of this world. If the official loses the post, there is no economic cushion on which he or she can fall back in the form of inherited wealth. The pleasant apartment, the second home in the country, the use of a government limousine, the access to special stores and high-quality closed medical services are all liable to vanish like confused images in a dream upon awakening in a cold harsh world. For high officials tenure in office appears to be at the pleasure of still higher officials. More concretely this means adherence to a political line constantly under-going subtle changes and, in addition, getting the proper results if the post involves the administration of economic affairs.

In 1959 Mervyn Matthews, a sociologist, concluded that there were just short of 400,000 managers of state administrative organizations and similar high level posts.[67] Undoubtedly the number is much larger now. This is the really privileged stratum of Soviet society. Under Brezhnev they managed to consolidate their position and enjoy their privileges to the point where one trenchant analyst wrote of 'supersta-bility' in the middle and late period of his rule.[68] For reasons to be discussed more fully in a moment, Brezhnev's rule may turn out to have been the golden age of the Soviet élite. Golden ages never last long. Quite apart from the matter of advancing age, new policies are likely at some point in the future to require new personnel.

Brezhnev's reign also coincided with a sharp rise in the number and importance of the professional stratum, a development that has its counterpart in advanced capitalist societies. Between 1965 and 1977 the number of specialists with higher and special middle education more than doubled, rising from a little over 12 million to more than 25 million. They included engineers, agronomists and veterinarians, eco-nomists, lawyers, and physicians. The proportion of specialists in the total labour force rose in these years from 15.7 per cent to almost a quarter, 23.7 per cent. The most interesting change is that for the first time this group became able to play a growing and important role in Soviet decision-making.[69] Presumably the specialists do this by pro-viding expert advice on specific situations and the prospects for alter-native policies. The political élite, it seems, still make the decisions and can reject the advice if they find it unpalatable or, perhaps more often, find another expert with more palatable advice. Though it would be as much of a gross exaggeration to speak of technocratic rule in the USSR as in the USA, the Brezhnev regime did display a professional–administrative ethos.[70] To me at least, this ethos gives off an odour that recalls American schools of public administration and business schools—morally earnest and conventional, technically proficient, and politically not very acute.

About the political and professional élites one often hears that the absence of inheritable private property on any very substantial scale is no bar to the transmission of privileged status to the next generation. According to this argument the children of educated couples have a much better chance of obtaining a university education than do the children of manual workers and peasants. The cultural atmosphere of the home in élite families is more stimulating and conducive to serious intellectual work. Finally, youngsters from privileged homes develop a range of personal contacts helpful in starting and sustaining careers that are not available to children from worker and peasant families.

All this is true, and there are some signs that it may become more true. But there remain important offsetting factors. Among the incumbents of élite specialist positions the share of individuals who came from a background of manual workers was reported in 1977 to be a third or more. In the late 1960s the relative share of working-class and peasant youths in the student bodies of several universities was about 30 per cent.[71] These figures indicate a very high degree of recruitment from workers and peasants. But there are important signs that the gate may be closing. In 1950–3 almost two-thirds of secondary school graduates gained admission to universities. Twenty years later the proportion had dropped to less than one in five.[72] On account of this there have been substantial disappointment and discontent among students whose aspirations for higher education and a corresponding career were blasted at an early age.[73] Should this trend continue, the élite might really turn into a mandarinate. On the other hand, the Party remains a channel for upward mobility for the politically ambitious with limited educational attainments. In 1976 slightly more than 30 per cent of the members of provincial and republican Party committees came from worker and peasant backgrounds.[74] Many of these may have been nominal or honorary workers and peasants. Yet 30 per cent is a goodly proportion, in fact the same as that of worker and peasant students in the universities.

Directors of large industrial enterprises in the late 1960s received 450–500 rubles a month in the Leningrad area. These were what is known as 'personal rates', that is, not a rate set for a particular job title but one granted to a particular individual with 'outstanding knowledge and experience in the field'. By this time such rates, set in excess of officially authorized ones for specific occupations, had become a 'mass phenomenon' for directors of large industrial enterprises.[75] Evidently the Soviet Union has been facing the same problem of attracting and holding first-rate managerial talent as that encountered in the United States. But the gap between managerial earnings and those of manual workers in the USSR is only a fraction of that which exists in the USA. Thus in the USSR the 'personal rates' of factory directors were around seven or eight times the legal minimum of 60 rubles a month at which cleaners were paid. Skilled workers were paid 141 rubles a month or between a third and a quarter of the director's earnings.[76] That is, of course, a very substantial set of inequalities, which have probably increased since the date of the study cited. But in the United States in 1981 higher paid executives received over 1.5 million dollars a year and a skilled worker in the order of $30,000 a year, which works out as a ratio of fifty to one.[77]

Soviet wages for manual workers in industry display considerable variation. In this area of the economy payment is mainly for the quantity and quality of work performed rather than in accord with the political and ethical considerations that govern payment at higher levels in the social system. Skill is rewarded by higher wages as is work in an industry granted high priority by the government.

Between 1955 and 1973, almost a generation, there has been a steadily declining relative advantage in the earnings of engineering technical personnel over those of manual workers. During this period the average monthly wages of manual workers nearly doubled, rising from 76.2 to 145.6 rubles a month. Engineering–technical personnel's earnings rose from 126.4 to only 184.9 rubles per month. In 1955 they earned 166 per cent of workers' wages. By 1973 the figure was down to 127 per cent.[78] For an especially privileged set of workers, those in coal mining, their average earnings in 1969 were higher than those received by the engineering–technical personnel in most of the other industries. The range of variation over all industries was from 210 rubles a month in coal mining down to 100 rubles a month in light industry.[79]

There was a reform of pay scales in 1964–5 that attempted to bring about a closer connection between remuneration and skill. The differentials between the lowest and the highest levels of remuneration after this reform came to 1:1.8 and 1:2.6, depending on the scale.[80] Thus it became possible for a skilled worker to earn nearly three times as much as an unskilled worker. Somewhat randomly chosen figures for Leningrad in the late 1960s and 1970 show a very much smaller

differential, one that might be exceptional. Skilled workers made 141
rubles a month and the unskilled 106.[81] A detailed analysis of official
wage scales and the methods used in drawing them up again reports a
much wider disparity, with skilled workers receiving two to three times
as much as unskilled. But it is not clear to what extent these differences corresponded to actual practice.[82]

There are some bits of evidence suggesting that in the early 1960s
about a third of the urban working class was poor by Soviet standards,
that is, their income was below 50 rubles per capita a month. As in
capitalist societies, such people were concentrated in unskilled and
semi-skilled occupations.[83] It seems likely that the proportion of the
poor diminished with the rise in living standards that took place under
Brezhnev.

Though wages are crucial for a worker, they are not everything in
life. The job also includes relationships with other workers and especially with the boss. In Stalin's day the boss tended to be a hard-driving
figure contemptuous in his language toward the workers. There are
signs that this situation had begun to change sharply in the 1960s. Ever
since Lenin's flirtation with Taylorism's time and motion studies,
Bolshevik leaders have displayed a strong interest in adapting capitalist
techniques of industrial management to socialist purposes. In the late
1960s and early 1970s, Soviet writers on factory management displayed a strong interest in the American 'human relations' approach.
How much of this approach seeped into actual Soviet practice is
difficult to discern.[84] Yet, if it does no more than reduce sharply the
crudity of the Soviet boss's treatment of workers—a crudity that, as
Lenin said, comes from turning ex-serfs into factory workers—it will
make life a lot pleasanter for industrial workers and probably raise
their productivity.

To a Western observer it may be somewhat surprising to learn that
in the USSR clerical and office employees, along with occupations
such as sales clerks that we label as white-collar jobs, rank for the most
part below manual labour in terms of both income and prestige. Thus
the monthly wages of clerical and office employees in the Leningrad
area in the late 1960s were only 90 rubles a month as against 106
rubles for unskilled manual workers and 141 for skilled manual
workers.[85] In what appear to be index numbers for the USSR as a
whole in 1973, workers' pay was rated as 100 and that of routine non-
manual workers at 84.5.[86] There is, however, evidence of considerable
geographical variation in the payment of white-collar workers as well

as those in other occupations. A Soviet study published in 1970, again using index numbers and this time with unskilled manual workers as 100, reported the earnings of 'other mental workers' (i.e., *not* skilled ones) as 85.7 for Leningrad, 102.6 for Kazan, 123.1 for Al'met'evsk, and 115.9 for Menzelinsk. The last three cities are in the Tatar Republic. If the 'other mental workers' were better paid than unskilled manual workers in these three cities, they nevertheless earned substantially less than skilled manual workers in all four cities.[87]

There appear to be two reasons for the lower position of the white-collar workers, or routine non-manual workers as Walter D. Connor calls them. First, the relatively higher wages of manual workers, and especially skilled manual workers, reflects the long-standing socialist preoccupation with the construction of heavy industry and the need to create incentives for this task. The second reason is that the routine non-manual jobs are for the most part filled by women.[88] Though this situation may be partly due to male prejudice, I do not think that is anything like the whole story. The workings of the labour market provide a better explanation. Routine non-manual tasks do not, as a rule, require as much physical strength as most forms of manual labour. Secondly, and most importantly, the women who do this work are often young and not yet married, or if they are married, they have husbands who earn more than they do. Rarely are these women heads of households. Since their earnings are merely auxiliary to those of a household, these women are willing and able to work for less. That of course is an old story under capitalism, an early phase of which is recapitulated here under socialism.

The degree of inequality in agriculture is very great too. A study of rural earnings in the Ukraine in 1970 found that collective farm chairmen earned 2,700 rubles a year while ordinary farm labourers earned only 531 rubles a year, a spread of about five to one. Soviet sources disagree as to whether earnings from the private plot diminish this inequality. Yanowitch estimates that such earnings could at most diminish the spread to three to one.[89] It is also likely that the peasants have been helped by the government's general policy of raising incomes at the bottom levels of Soviet society. Peasants are now included in the social security system. In addition, collective farms are now covered by a state insurance system against bad harvests.[90]

Nevertheless, as the figures on rural income show clearly, socialist agriculture is burdened by very heavy administrative costs. In addition to the chairman (2,700 rubles) there are chief specialists (1,935 rubles), work-brigade leaders and heads of livestock departments (1,268 rubles), agronomists (1,260 rubles), tractor operators, motor vehicle drivers (1,081 rubles), office and store-keeping personnel (780 rubles). All of these may in some sense be necessary for agricultural operations. Clearly the tractor drivers are. Nevertheless, they add up to a very large overhead, all of which eventually comes out of peasant earnings and serves to depress them. The old saying that the Russian peasant pays for everything is no longer true in an industrialized economy. But he still pays for a great deal.

4

CHINA*

THE comparative theme of these studies makes it appropriate to use the Soviet Union as a grid for viewing China. Therefore I shall emphasize the ways in which China resembles and differs from the Soviet Union. At the same time the comparative emphasis should not become a Procrustean frame that obliterates unique yet crucial features of the Chinese experience.

1 Dynastic society and abortive liberal impulses

In the latter part of the nineteenth century both Russia and China were huge continental powers, each governed by bureaucracies nominally under the control of an autocratic emperor. In China, much more than in Russia, access to the bureaucracy was a function of merit. In China merit was demonstrated in the form of literary skill. To acquire this skill took time freed from other work, especially manual labour, which in turn implies the ownership of a substantial amount of landed property by one's parents or sometimes an unrelated benefactor. In the Russian bureaucracy there was an emphasis on military qualities and manners, quite lacking in the imperial Chinese bureaucracy.

The imperial authorities ruled over populations that were overwhelmingly peasant. In both societies peasant rebellion was endemic, a fact which suggests that many peasants did not perceive their overlords as performing any necessary or useful social function. Beyond the similarity of an intermittently turbulent peasant mass, there were very significant differences. To my knowledge no one has yet explored the consequences and meaning of these differences. I can only report them very briefly. Russian peasant agriculture was extensive and inefficient in the sense of using large amounts of land for relatively small yields. Wheat was the principal crop. In many parts of Russia the peasants also had in the village community a strong

*Note on transliteration of Chinese: Since several of the sources cited, including recently published ones, still use the Wade-Giles system instead of the contemporary pinyin, I have thought it less confusing to use whichever system the cited author used.

collective organization. By contrast, Chinese agriculture was intensive and very efficient in its use of labour. One reason may be that only some ten per cent of the area of China is suitable for cultivation. In contrast to the Russian village community Chinese peasant society tended strongly toward individualism based on privately owned plots. The contrast, however, needs to be shaded a bit. Peasants were brought into co-operative networks in two major ways. One was through share-cropping, widely practised throughout China. The other was the clan, a religiously based lineage group that flourished mainly in the more prosperous southern half of China. (The South grew rice; the North, wheat and millet.) The activities of the clan were religious, moral, educational, and economic, including—it is claimed—assistance to less well-to-do members.

Chinese town-dwellers present some puzzles that make generalization difficult. Modern research has, so far as I can see, quite destroyed the notion that Imperial China was like Imperial Russia, a land of administrative cities and hence a land without a bourgeoisie or, more accurately, without merchants. China had a great many merchants. Many cities were commercial centres. Urban centres of varied size and importance dotted large parts of the Chinese countryside. They were not confined to the coastal areas.[1] Scholars now point to an urban medieval revolution, that occurred between 900 and 1300 in different parts of China, evidently fueled by merchant activity. It resulted in the expansion of some walled cities, the growth of commercial suburbs outside their gates, the emergence of numerous small and intermediate towns, and other changes.[2]

On the other hand, in China this mercantile class had neither the cultural nor political effects that its counterpart had in Western Europe or even to a considerably lesser extent in Tokugawa Japan. In China distinctive cultural traits appear to have been minimal or altogether lacking, as the bureaucratic and landholding élite accepted and absorbed the merchants.[3] Another authority tells us that 'no Chinese communities ever established themselves as municipalities possessing defined powers of independent jurisdiction'.[4] That of course stands in the sharpest possible contrast with urban developments in the West toward the end of the Middle Ages. Indeed, the absence of separate urban jurisdictions is enough to render the term bourgeoisie inapplicable to China.

There is a great difficulty here in trying to explain why the Chinese merchants—and artisans, another important element in the urban population—failed to undertake any serious drive to share in political power when their economic base apparently made such an attempt quite feasible. Two considerations come to mind. First the merchants may have acquired as much power as they wanted at the local level as wealthier elements became absorbed into the local gentry.[5] Secondly, there were, it seems to me, limits to this process of absorption, set up by the landed bureaucratic élite. These men tended to be quite jealous of any system of social ranking, such as money, that could challenge the basis of their own system of rank and precedence, which rested on intellectual merit as demonstrated by success in examinations. For this reason they opposed, and generally successfully, other sources of prestige, including medicine. Only when the imperial system as a whole began to break down, in the nineteenth century, did this resistance gradually cease to be effective. This mixture of resistance and limited absorption by an élite of scholar-bureaucrats and wealthy landholders may have been the reason why there was no 'bourgeois' political impulse and no strong drive for liberal democracy in Imperial China.

In Tsarist Russia, peasant rebellions had been put down by force of arms. In China such rebellions might help to overturn a dynasty. But they could not or would not on their own introduce a new social order. With the coming of the twentieth century the peasants in China gained leadership from disaffected urban intellectuals and some help from workers in the cities. In combination with other historically unique factors to be discussed shortly, these new elements enabled a revolutionary movement to take power and keep it.

In reviewing the pre-modern social development of the Russian and Chinese Empires, we can see that the institutional seedlings that in Western Europe were to produce liberal democracy were stunted or nearly altogether absent. But in China there were some different seedlings that faced different obstacles. As already pointed out, in China the merchant influences had long been held in check by the scholar–gentry state, which feared the morally corrosive effects of mere wealth on the system of status and social inequality that supported the whole edifice. As the Chinese state crumbled in the latter half of the nineteenth century, commerce and industry passed to a great extent into foreign hands.

In the Chinese countryside there is, at least in Western sources, hardly any sign of the vigorous village community and its assembly that was so important in managing peasant affairs in Russia. What clues there are refer to the situation in quite ancient times, long before the establishment of the Empire. A Soviet scholar, referring to events before Confucius (died c. 468 BC), claims to have found evidence for a village assembly, consisting of the heads of groups of five households, and a council of elders. Both bodies were chosen by the community as a whole and served as the main local authority.[6] I suspect that this claim may reflect the myths of Engels and Chinese tradition more than ancient Chinese social realities. Nevertheless, it is plain that the general idea of ordinary people coming together to discuss critically the policies of the ruler did exist in ancient China. A well-known chronicle purporting to report events of 542 BC reports: 'The people of Cheng were in the habit of discussing the administration of the state when they gathered at leisure in the village schools'. For this reason someone suggested to the ruler that it might be a good idea to close the schools. But the ruler rejected this proposal, saying in effect that popular criticism helped him to encourage good policies and correct bad ones.[7] Like so much Chinese political discussion, right down to the present day, this little report has a didactic and moralizing tone. It is almost impossible to tell what social practices if any lay behind it. But it does demonstrate the existence of democratic ideas in some quarters that included the peasantry.

For reasons about which I have to confess ignorance, this tradition of peasant self-government, never apparently very strong, died out. There is scarcely a trace of it in classical Chinese philosophy, which is mainly political philosophy, that began with Confucius and ended with the founding of the Empire in 221 BC. Bounding forward through the centuries to the Southern Sung (1127–1279), we learn that village affairs were run by well-to-do and literate landowners appointed by the state. Appointment to this form of state service was a highly unpopular burden, partly because the main task was collecting taxes.[8] There is no indication of participation by the peasants. Under the last dynasty, the Ch'ing (1644–1912), there was, on the other hand, at least minimum token representation in the form of a supposedly elected headman or set of headmen for the village as well as basic rural division (*hsiang*) and town (*chen*). In an attempt to prevent undue autonomy on the part of the headmen the central government also imposed its own tax collection and local security system on the villages and other localities. Since the district magistrate, the bottom official on the bureaucratic ladder and the local representative of imperial authority, had responsibility for between 100,000 and over 250,000 people,[9] it is highly probable that the headman had a good deal of freedom of action. How many of them were peasants is another matter, since the government wanted to rest its authority on men of *Besitz und Bildung*, just as most governments do sooner or later. But there are seldom enough of such men to go around, and a scattering of the more prosperous peasants with political talents may well have found room to exercise them locally. If, on the other hand, they were really ambitious, with some talent for book learning, they would find support for the route that led to the examination hall and the Imperial service instead of strictly local intrigues.

If we turn our eyes from the mass of the population and look instead at the Imperial institution, we do find some ideas and practices that contained a liberal democratic potential. One is the familiar Mandate of Heaven, under which the Emperor ruled, and which included the right of rebellion in case of severe misrule. One excellent scholar has remarked: 'The idea that the people had the right to rebel against oppressive rule remained at the heart of Chinese dynastic politics until the twentieth century . . . '.[10] At least they had the right if they won. It is important that this was a right of rebellion, not of revolution. There was no idea of changing the political system or the social order. The idea of revolution took a long time to develop in the West and would have been anachronistic in Imperial China. Nevertheless, a right of rebellion obviously implies a right to resist unjust and arbitrary authority under roughly specifiable circumstances.

There is another aspect of the Chinese imperial system that does have strong theoretical affinities with Western liberalism, though there is almost certainly no historical connection between the two. That is the right of remonstrance, which evidently existed as early as the Book of Odes, composed around 600 BC, or nearly four centuries before the founding of the Empire. The essential idea was that an adviser to a ruler had both a right and an obligation to give unpalatable advice to the ruler. The general content of such advice emphasized policies that would bring material benefits to the underlying population. Hence a ruler should avoid policies of military aggrandizement and glory as well as heavy expenses for parks, imposing buildings, and other forms of luxurious display. All these ideas may be found in Mencius (372 to *c.* 288 BC) and in sketchier form in other classical philosophers.

The tradition remained alive down to the end of the Empire, undergoing changes in response to changing circumstances. The difficulty was that the right of remonstrance was little more than an ethical tradition. There was no interest group to back it up or force an unwilling Emperor to follow advice against his own inclinations. Nevertheless, occasional advisers with more courage than sense of self-preservation tried to put the idea into effect.[11] Much later the idea of legitimate dissent and the myths that had become attached to dissenting acts turned into a harmless, romantic, and self-pitying symbolism that could comfort those exiled from the court.[12] Finally under the last dynasty, the Ch'ing, the Censorate, a body theoretically bound to guide and admonish even the Emperor himself, became in practice little more than a body of secret agents providing him with secret information on civil and military officials at all levels.[13] Thus what might have been the origin of a system of loyal opposition, the keystone of liberal democracy, under the specific conditions of Imperial China became a form of secret police. Further comments on the prospects for liberal democracy in traditional China are superfluous.

2 Contrasts with Russia in the revolutionary road to power

The road to power for the Russian and the Chinese Communists was quite different, a set of differences that had important consequences for their subsequent methods of rule. Taking advantage of a surge of support among the urban workers, a tiny but strategic minority of the population, the Russian Bolsheviks carried out a coup and took control of the capital. From there they extended their power outward, neutralizing the peasantry with the promise of land and putting down organized opposition by force of arms. There is no sign that the Bolsheviks ever enjoyed widespread support throughout Russia.

The Chinese Communists came to power in 1949 through victory in what amounted to a prolonged civil war with the Kuomintang. The fact of war meant that the Chinese Red Army, later known as the People's Liberation Army, was the decisive instrument of victory. As a highly politicized army, it was a very remarkable instrument, though we have precious little information about its internal workings for this early period. Somehow Mao Tse-tung was able to take rag-tag semi-bandits, men torn loose from their social roots who furnished recruits for war-lords and the Kuomintang as well, and transform them into a highly disciplined fighting force. As part of their training the soldiers learned not to copy the Kuomintang brutal treatment of the peasants. Instead, by and large, they treated peasant property and persons with respect, an astonishing contrast with the behaviour of both Kuomintang and traditional men under arms. It seems to me that this transformation of the soldiery from the most unpromising raw material into a politicized yet effective fighting force must have contributed heavily to Mao's subsequent faith in the possibility of transforming human nature in accord with socialist ideals.

By the late 1940s the Kuomintang in its decay toward a regime of near-gangsters had come to alienate almost everybody. In contrast, the Chinese Communist Party enjoyed some support among all sectors of Chinese society: peasants, partly because the Party soft-pedaled land reforms while offering protection from landlords and officials under the wing of the Kuomintang; intellectuals, workers, and even some capitalists tired of Kuomintang thuggery and disenchanted by the apparent weakness of its resistance to Japan. This combination of factors makes it appear that the Chinese Communists triumphed because they offered a more appealing social programme and were more honest and fair in their relationships with the population. That is an important part of the truth. But it is only a part.

First of all, during the war the Japanese gained control of the coastal (and modern) areas of China where the Kuomintang had been strongest. Thereby, the Japanese deprived the Kuomintang of its main base of social support and of its revenues. This fact alone goes a long way toward explaining the increasingly exploitative behaviour of Kuomintang officials in the parts of China still under their control.

Elsewhere, in response to the Japanese occupation, Kuomintang officials and landlords moved out of the countryside and into the towns, leaving the peasants to their own devices. Then the Japanese army's intermittent mopping up and extermination campaigns tended to weld the peasants into an emotionally united mass. Thus the Japanese helped to perform two essential revolutionary tasks for the Chinese Communists: the elimination of old élites and the forging of solidarity among the oppressed.

Turning now to straightforward military factors, we learn that the Kuomintang armies did suffer very heavy losses in their occasional battles with the Japanese. At this point we begin to perceive the Kuomintang as a 'ruling' party deprived of troops, money, and social support, mainly as a consequence of Japanese actions. Finally, in the closing stages of the war the Russians turned over to the Chinese Communists a large amount of arms and supplies that they had taken from the Japanese in Manchuria. According to Max Beloff, 'these arms . . . must supply the reason why the [Chinese] Communist forces, so poorly armed before the autumn of 1945, appeared to be so well provided in the subsequent campaigns'.[14]

Thus the Chinese Communists were very fortunate in having the unintentional assistance of the Japanese in destroying their main rival and, at the end of the war, obtaining through the Russians Japanese arms to finish them off. I can see no way to assess the relative importance of this Japanese assistance in relation to their own programme and efforts to establish a foothold except to notice one important fact: the Chinese Communists were unable to take and hold a territorial base until after the Japanese conquest was far advanced. On balance, then, it seems that the Chinese Communists' political and military strategy was a far less important ingredient in their success than the unwitting help they received from the Japanese. It is also important to stress, as the Chinese Communist leaders themselves have done, that the final stage of the Civil War was one of full-scale battles, with history if not God on the side of the better armed troops. This set of considerations suggests the conclusion that in other countries Communist–Nationalist guerrilla movements have not yet uncovered a foolproof political and military formula for overthrowing even a decayed and oppressive *ancien régime*. More succinctly, popular support by itself cannot guarantee revolutionary success.

3 *Political institutions after the revolution*

When the Chinese Communists came to power in 1949, their administrative apparatus was a highly decentralized one, reflecting the military situation during the Civil War. There were seven liberated areas, each ruled by a military control committee. Though the Party guaranteed unity of a sort, such a loose structure obviously would not do for a Party dedicated to introducing a new social order, even if the date of the new order's arrival was uncertain. It took a surprisingly long time to hammer out a new set of political institutions, amid very keen competition for a much smaller number of much more important posts than had existed under the system of regional military control commissions. After five years, or in 1954, however, the transformation began in earnest.[15]

The political institutions that emerged were a rough copy of those in the Soviet Union. For the purposes at hand there is no use in attempting a complete list, partly because a good many changes have occurred, and more significantly, because our interest is in issues that persist despite such changes. Nevertheless, a brief sketch of the major institutions that have displayed a moderate shelf-life so far may make the subsequent analysis easier to follow.

First and foremost is of course the Communist Party, which runs or sets policy for just about every aspect of social life. Until very recently the Politburo has been the decision-making nucleus for the Party, dealing with all big issues and many small ones. The role of the Central Committee, a much larger body, is less clear. To some extent it seems to be a necessary source of legitimacy for decisions by the Politburo, and thus a potential check on the Politburo. It may also issue some policy decisions and recommendations on its own.

The State Council stands between the top Party leadership and the government ministries, and possesses a set of departments corresponding to these ministries. (The arrangement recalls Stalin's secretariat which was a miniature of the Soviet government, though China's State Council is probably more independent.) It has on several occasions issued orders jointly with the Party's Central Committee. In 1957 at the height of China's brief experiment in freedom of criticism, known as the Hundred Flowers movement, critics asserted that the State Council was the root of bureaucratism in the new state.[16]

The State Council is not formally a Party organization. Neither of course are the government ministries (and commissions, such as the State Planning Commission) that the State Council presumably supervises—or at least several of which it presumably supervises. These ministries are at least formally in charge of a wide range of economic and political functions, such as agriculture, several branches of industry, national defence, police, and many others. The control of a ministry is assured after a fashion by appointing Party members to key posts and by the Politburo's efforts to keep an eye on what is going on everywhere. Competition and jealousy on the part of other ministries almost certainly provides a flow of information upward, most of it hostile, which the top Party leaders can use in deciding whether to strengthen a specific ministry or clip its wings.

In theory, the National People's Congress is the supreme legislative authority, though it is hard to conceive of that body's acting in any way contrary to the wishes of a resolute majority of the Party Politburo. The first such Congress was held in 1954. As part of the establishment of the new political apparatus just described it created what appears to be a quite important body, the Standing Committee. This act appears to have been an early attempt to set limits on Mao's exuberance and impetuosity. No longer could Mao enact and interpret laws, promulgate decrees, and supervise their execution on his own. Henceforth, he could promulgate laws and decrees only in accordance with the decisions of the National People's Congress or, when that was not in session, the Standing Committee. According to the new system, the Standing Committee was interposed between Mao and the major administrative organs that had just been created. Thus the Standing Committee became responsible for supervision of the day-to-day workings of the Cabinet, the Defence Council, the Supreme Court, and other offices. Since such an important figure as Liu Shao-ch'i was chairman of the Standing Committee, it is plain that top Party leaders took on this task of daily supervision.[17]

The National People's Congress is not elected directly. It is chosen by the next lower level of congresses and is thus twice or thrice removed from direct popular election. Only the basic level congresses are directly elected by the people. They hold an impressive list of formal powers, similar to those of local soviets in the USSR, of which they are the approximate counterpart. But, as in the USSR, they are not at all independent bodies. Their task is to carry out tasks assigned by higher councils. They are 'subordinate to and under the direction of the State Council'.[18]

If in theory the National People's Congress is the supreme legislative authority, what is it in practice? My impression is that its power to initiate important legislation or policy on its own is null. Apparently the function of this Congress has been to cast a cloak of legitimacy over policies and institutional changes that have first been thrashed out among top Party leaders elsewhere. When a predominant faction in the Party has wanted to do something, they go ahead and do it anyway, using all levers of persuasion and coercion at their command, but without bothering about the National People's Congress. When the dust has cleared they may or may not call a session of the National People's Congress to ratify the policy, if it has been moderately successful, or to patch up the tattered rags covering the nakedness of autocratic power, if the damage has been severe, as it was following the Cultural Revolution.[19]

4 Reasons for the growth of socialist bureaucracy

This set of political innovations added up to the deliberate creation of an imposing bureaucratic edifice. By 1958 there were almost 8,000,000 state cadres in China. Ten years earlier the Kuomintang, who never managed to control the whole country, employed some

2,000,000 state functionaries.[20] The Ch'ing empire in the nineteenth century had only about 40,000 official posts.[21] Presumably for good and sufficient reasons, the Chinese Communists after a long and bloody struggle replaced the bureaucratic apparatus of pre-modern China with their own version, some two hundred times larger.

If the reasons were good and sufficient, they were not necessarily compelling to all the top Party leadership and especially not to Mao. Though he was often very pragmatic, there was also a strong egalitarian and populist streak in him. By 1957 his greatest concern—and a long standing one—was with human relations between rulers and ruled. He was 'primarily critical of bureaucratic distance from the people and failure to deal adequately with their needs'.[22] These concerns set Mao sharply apart from Stalin. In the 1930s, as we have seen, Stalin came out bluntly against 'equality mongering'. In his famous and endlessly repeated slogan, 'Cadres decide everything', Stalin came out equally bluntly in favour of bureaucracy. Not until after Mao's death would a similar slogan put in an appearance in China.[23] In the USSR, if bureaucrats were to be criticized or shot, that was because Stalin or one of his close associates wanted them removed from the scene. There was to be no attack on bureaucracy as such. Stalin resolved the moral dilemma of socialism so decisively that he just about made it disappear. On the other hand, Mao's uneasiness enables us to see the issue much more clearly, as well as the near impossibility of an egalitarian and populist resolution. In order to carry out the transition to socialism in an economically backward country, it is necessary to establish and set in motion a large bureaucratic apparatus of persuasion and coercion. Marx, it may be remarked parenthetically, did not perceive the need for this apparatus of persuasion and coercion because he expected the natural evolution of capitalism to generate revolutionary mass support for a socialist society. Furthermore, the concentration of capital into ever larger units would create the necessary machinery and levers of command for 'the people' to step in and run them as a socialist society. Instead it has been necessary to create the industrial base under the auspices of a command economy.

Is it possible, on the other hand, to dismount the command economy once socialism has been established? The answer, I believe, is that it is just barely possible, but highly unlikely, and that the result would be the end of socialism. In any modern economy it is necessary to find ways to produce a specific mix of goods and services and to distribute

these goods and services among the population. There are really only
two ways of doing this. One is through the mechanisms of the free
market, or, if one rejects the workings of the market on moral and
political grounds, one has to use a system of bureaucratic commands to
oversee and co-ordinate production and consumption throughout the
society. As one economist put the point, in arguing against the youthful
rebels of the sixties and seventies, one can be against the market or
against bureaucracy. But if one is against both of them, one is in real
intellectual trouble.[24]

In static pre-industrial and pre-commercial societies there is a third
way of co-ordinating economic activities that we can call custom.
Examples are available in the practice of medieval peasants who
performed labour services on the overlord's land and perhaps brought
him a chicken at specific times in the year. The exchanges of the Kula
ring in the Trobriands, made familiar by Bronislaw Malinowski, are
another well-known example. But custom can only be an effective
guide to behaviour in a society that changes very little over long periods
of time. Otherwise custom ceases to be effective, as groups and
individuals struggle to preserve or improve their position. Hence
custom as such cannot provide a guiding mechanism for production
and exchange in a modern economy.

If we are left with the choice between co-ordination of the economy
through the market or by bureaucratic command, what are the possibilities of combining the two systems? More specifically, how should
we assess China's current attempts to use the market to eliminate or
circumvent the shortcomings and inefficiencies of socialism?

As in the Soviet Union, these 'reformist' programmes arouse the
hostility of Communists with strong feelings about the general wicked-
ness of markets and of bureaucrats who fear that their functions may
become superfluous under the proposed changes. Opposition from
such sources will inevitably be very powerful, though not necessarily
insuperable. Fundamentally this opposition is correct from the standpoint of a commitment to socialism. At bottom the issue is one of
power, what Lenin called tersely 'who [beats] whom'. If a really
important section of this bureaucracy were to break loose from socialist
controls and follow market cues, all the other sections would be
affected. We can imagine what would happen if the section of the
bureaucracy responsible for oil production and marketing went its own
way in search of domestic and foreign markets. Socialism as a whole

would begin to unravel. For these reasons we may conclude that socialist bureaucracies are here to stay, with relatively minor modifications.

5 *Purposes and techniques of bureaucratic control*

The purpose of the bureaucratic apparatus in China and elsewhere is not merely to control the economy but also to control and remould the day-to-day behaviour and even the thoughts of the people. To this end the Chinese Communists have used a system of mutual surveillance and enforced indoctrination by means of small groups of between eight and fifteen in number—large enough to exert strong pressure on the individual but small enough to remain a face-to-face group—that have no real parallel in the Soviet Union. Pre-figurings may be found at times in systems of mutual responsibility for reporting and limiting undesired or criminal behaviour in Imperial China, especially toward the end of the last dynasty. However, the Imperial measures seem to have been quite ineffective. Therefore, the modern system of small-group control, which extends Big Brother's influence down to the grass roots, appears to be an adaptation of an old, unsuccessful social device, with its stricter supervision from above and its greater emphasis on thought control. From what takes place in these small groups as now organized in China we can see that the small-group controls are an attempt to apply populist ideas to the problems of domination and management of the underlying population.

So far as possible, the Chinese authorities try to insert every individual into a small group based on mutual surveillance. It is not very difficult to keep them there because migration and job-changing are subject to strict controls. If one or more individuals need to have their thoughts remoulded, something that happens very often on account of incessant political campaigns and frequent changes in the Party line, suitable 'study' materials are provided, namely authoritative government pronouncements and, more rarely, something comprehensible from the Marxist classics. The group leader reads the text and then calls for questions. Here occurs a dangerous moment. Everybody has to say something, but anything one says is likely to reveal 'bad thoughts'. Bad thoughts may also come out in the most casual conversation or piece of unintentional behaviour that seems anti-social. Then comes a hail of criticism from other group members. The victim feels, at the very least, utterly humiliated and bereft of all social support. There is nothing to be done except stand quietly and confess guilt.

Curiously enough, none of the group members may believe what they say. But the group pressure is enough to make them go through with the ritual. At most one of them may say later and privately—if possible —the equivalent of 'Sorry, old chap; we gave you a hard time': to which the accepted reply is a deprecatory shrug of the shoulders.

A relatively severe and humiliating hail of criticism is called a 'struggle meeting'. The struggle meeting also occurs outside the context of the small group, in which case the victim has to face a large crowd hurling insults and invective. Though most struggle meetings stop short of physical abuse, quite a number, especially during the Cultural Revolution, went on to beating and killing the victim. Psychological collapse and subsequent suicide have also been common. Partial statistics on the number of deaths during the Cultural Revolution, released as part of the attack on the Gang of Four, claim 34,000 fatalities in Yenan (Yanan) and Inner Mongolia, with a figure of 12,000 for Peking (Beijing) alone.[25]

To return to the small group, any Western male who has been subject as a youngster to intense bullying is likely to recognize the fear, loss of self-esteem, and at least temporary willingness to accept the moral standards of the bullies, that such an episode can produce. But because such bullies are in some sense foreigners and outsiders for the Western victim, that experience is easier to bear than savage criticism by work-mates and neighbours. The main factors that make the Chinese system of small-group controls effective are (1) the threat of withdrawing group support, leaving the individual, so to speak, naked and afraid and (2) active punishment by the group for violation of its rules. The viciousness of the struggle meeting recalls the remarks of the anthropologist Clyde Kluckhohn about the way human beings enjoy the luxury of legitimate aggression. If the Chinese Communists have not been able to provide luxury for the masses in the form of food, they have deliberately and freely provided it in the form of legitimate aggression.

The effectiveness of small-group mutual surveillance depends on the effectiveness of larger groups in encapsulating the individual. In the gaol where Bao Ruowang (Jean Pasqualini) was incarcerated for some time, its effectiveness was remarkable in preventing the development of an inmates' subculture of the kind that prevails in Western gaols. There appears to be a sharp contrast too with Stalinist gaols. Former inmates of these have observed that the gaol was the freest place in Russia because the guards paid no attention to what inmates talked about.

Apparently, the little group of Bao's cell-mates indoctrinated one another to the point of complete compliance with the authorities' demands and even considerable internalization of the required norms.[26]

At the opposite extreme, these small groups temporarily atrophied during the Cultural Revolution when the supporting bureaucratic framework disintegrated.[27] The Cultural Revolution was of course a time when large struggle groups burst out all over. In a rough sense and for a limited time they replaced the mutual surveillance groups, which, however, returned as the Cultural Revolution subsided. Between these extremes of nearly perfect effectiveness and rare atrophy there are many degrees of effectiveness. By and large small groups seem to work quite well in maintaining social control over behaviour even when little thought reform takes place.[28]

6 Corruption, the mass line, and public criticism

At this point we may turn to the defects and shortcomings in the Chinese Communist system of bureaucratic authority and the Party's efforts to overcome them. Most of the information on such matters comes from what some Party officials think is wrong. That is a limitation to be kept in mind. The Party airs only the dirty linen that it selects. Such decisions, to be more precise, are part of the perpetual factional struggles. An official tries to air a rival's dirty linen, not his own. His own defects he will expose only in connection with the public humiliation of a struggle meeting, an event which of course signalizes defeat in a factional contest. Nevertheless, if some powerful Party officials point to a particular bureaucratic malpractice as a serious matter, we can be reasonably sure that it really is a serious problem. And if the complaints are widespread and persist over time, there are grounds for suspecting that they reflect endemic defects.*

Before examining the defects and shortcomings that are the subject of frequent and intense public criticism I want to mention one defect that no Chinese official would be likely to cite publicly. Since its early days, the Chinese Communist regime has been a government by

*Exposing a rival's shortcomings in order to disgrace that person is probably a universal aspect of factional infighting. It occurs in the royal courts of pre-industrial socieites, contemporary capitalist governments of all shades, large business firms, and of course other socialist governments. What distinguishes factional conflict in socialist and fascist regimes from others is, I suggest, the combination of secrecy, vindictiveness, and savage penalties for failure. Yet even on these counts the differences are matters of degree.

campaigns. It is a series of never-ending mobilizations to arouse the enthusiasm or the indignation of the masses. With the passage of time and the defeat of some shining hopes (such as the Great Leap Forward, discussed briefly later) both the enthusiasm and the indignation probably become increasingly synthetic. It is necessary to be cautious in such judgements because it is very difficult to assess the feelings of a crowd, especially one that has already become part of history. While clearly obvious in China, government by campaign is characteristic of totalitarian regimes generally. Continually changing targets of enthusiastic acclaim or indignant condemnation provide useful flexibility. They are also useful symbolic bows toward rule by the people in an age when ruling élites can no longer afford to be explicitly anti-democratic.

Without undue oversimplification one can reduce the flow of public criticism of the Chinese Communist bureaucracy to two main charges. First of all, it is claimed, the bureaucracy is exceedingly corrupt. In the second place, it is arbitrary in the exercise of power, being unresponsive not only to the people whom it is expected to serve but also the leaders whom it is required to obey. To correct such defects the regime has used the following devices. It has subjected erring desk-bound bureaucrats to a dose of manual labour and contact with the masses. Early on, the regime had developed the theory and practice of the mass line (discussed later), supposedly a way of ascertaining and executing the popular will. In addition it has developed a punitive system of public criticism of bureaucrats. China under Mao, in comparison with the Soviet Union, begins to look like an awkward attempt to set up a form of populist totalitarianism, hardly a feasible objective since popular demands are so often contradictory. After Mao's death, the populist elements, especially those with a punitive edge toward officialdom, receded into the background.

Since the defects of the bureaucracy and the regime's efforts to overcome them—as well as its perception of what really is a defect—form the living tissue of authority and inequality in China, it is necessary to examine them in some detail. Corruption is a good theme with which to begin. It has been rife in the Chinese Communist bureaucracy practically ever since the Party came to power. The distortions of bureaucracy were already a focus of major political campaigns in 1950 and 1953. In 1951 there was a scandal about two Party secretaries in Tientsin who lived a 'decadent life and engaged extensively in illegal business with state funds'.[29] Such scandals have remained a prominent part of the political landscape down to the present day.[30] Around 1962 corruption in the countryside was 'still' a serious problem. This was the kind that affected most people since it had to do with collective farm accounts and work points or, in other words, a basic source of the peasants' income.[31]

Some of the main sources of this corruption, to be described in further detail in a moment, are not difficult to discern. They afflict all economically backward socialist societies, though in varying degrees, and for that matter not just the socialist ones. In the first place, the Chinese Communists created a very large bureaucracy very rapidly, without adequate training or suitable traditions. A high proportion of bureaucrats are still 'technically incompetent *apparatchiki* and superannuated guerrilla leaders'.[32] In outlook and behaviour they are about as far as possible from Max Weber's scrupulously objective bureaucratic official. Instead their behaviour derives from personal connections and gifts from an applicant seeking some kind of authorization. Again based on personal connections, but also with an eye on the everchanging Party line, he has to determine whether granting or refusing the authorization would be most helpful to his status in the bureaucratic hierarchy.[33]

The most recent example that has come to my attention reveals some holes in the network of bureaucratic controls (and recalls textbook descriptions of customs barriers and tax collectors in France of the *ancien régime*). On China's rare, special high-speed automobile highways, various organizations, not further identified, set themselves up at various points along the highways to collect tolls. This they did without any authorization at all. The situation got so far out of hand that individuals were passing themselves off as 'administrative personnel' to collect tolls. We learn this from a directive of the Council of State, dated 5 July 1985, forbidding these practices and announcing that only policemen and members of the traffic control organizations in uniform could collect tolls. Evidently there are many other illegal ways of collecting illegal fees and taxes. Probably they are more remunerative. In one city, for example, several institutions (again not further defined) imposed fees on behalf of what they called a health administration. These fees were so high that they put some private firms out of business.[34]

Though there are tendencies toward venality, favouritism, and an eye toward the main chance in even the most 'incorruptible' bureaucracies of economically advanced states, such tendencies are especially blatant in China. At any rate the top leaders think so. In August 1964 Mao made a disenchanted comment on these traits that has often been quoted. Asserting that the enemy, i.e., bureaucrats, had taken over a third of the state, he went on to claim:

At present you can buy a [Party] branch secretary for a few packs of cigarettes, not to mention marrying a daughter to him.[35]

Mao was concerned primarily with low-level corruption, which of course affected the people most. Around the same time Liu Shao-ch'i asserted that Mao's estimate of the situation was too cheerful. According to Liu, 30 per cent of all cadres were bad and another 40 per cent mediocre. In a large number of rural areas they waved the Communist flag but in reality served the Kuomintang.[36] Since Liu was much closer to day-to-day administrative problems than Mao, his remarks, even if exaggerated, deserve attention.

Another reason for corruption in addition to the shortage of adequate personnel, and one that afflicts non-socialist states that are economically backward as well as socialist ones, is the bureaucracy's near monopoly of the good things in life. In a situation of widespread scarcity, where the bureaucracy controls the allocation of goods and services, rewards and penalties, just about the only way to get material goods and improved social status is through or in the bureaucracy. As the American sociologist William Graham Sumner said around the turn of the century, 'If you live in a country run by a committee, get on the committee'. Not every ambitious and inventive individual can hope to succeed in this aim, even if he or she is very skilled at social manipulation. Capitalist societies have tried with no little success to make socially constructive use of the somewhat unattractive traits of acquisitiveness, personal as opposed to collective ambition, and aptness for social manipulation. In a socialist society these traits, especially acquisitiveness, are in bad odour, while a bureaucracy provides temptation for their display. Hence especially though not exclusively in a socialist society these traits flourish like cockroaches in the damp cracks and dark interstices of the prevailing morality.

To combat the major defects of their bureaucracy, corruption and 'commandism', or the use of orders backed up by brute force instead of persuasion, the Chinese Communists have developed a number of practices that reflect their anti-élitist sentiments. One of these is a stint of manual labour, sometimes combined with demotion, for erring bureaucrats. Speaking of cadres, Mao asserted, 'The problems of corruption and enjoying more benefits can be resolved only when there is participation in labour'.[37] For Maoists, manual labour and mixing with the masses is supposed to be uplifting and morally purifying. Such ideas may be a deliberate or unconscious revolutionary reversal of those held by the dominant classes in Imperial times.[38] However, there is also a practical side to this moral injunction. Direct contact with the masses can enable a bureaucrat to see the problems ordinary people face and the real obstacles to executing official policies. On this score, the difficulty of course is that officials are so overloaded with tasks and paper work that they can seldom if ever get out of their offices.

After the victory of 1949 the first official mention of this device of participation in labour that I have come upon is a directive of the Party Central Committee of 27 April 1957 that 'called for the systematization of participation in labor by leading Party, government, and army personnel'.[39] Shortly afterward, in February 1958, the total number of cadres demoted to production or lower-level leadership posts reached 1.3 million. In the spring of 1958 another million cadres were sent off for a year's labour.[40] Evidently the Party leaders were deadly serious about using this device, at least at this moment. So far as I am aware, on the other hand, the experiment was not tried again on this scale for some time. The next major attempt to enforce such policies came with the establishment of the May 7th Cadre Schools, named after Mao's directive of 7 May 1966 during the Cultural Revolution. Part of the idea behind the directive was an attempt to overcome rigid occupational specialization by compelling individuals to experience at least temporarily a different working environment. But in practice the schools seemed to have been a ritualized farce. Urban officials when sent down to May 7th Cadre Schools 'retained their high incomes as they steeped themselves in revolutionary spirit by working temporarily in the countryside'.[41] To judge from continuing complaints about corruption and other evils, the device of temporary participation in manual labour has had virtually no effect.

Another major device for keeping bureaucracy under control is the theory and practice of the mass line. To call it a device is somewhat of an understatement since it is really a theory of how the Party ought to rule. As such it sharply distinguishes the Chinese from the Russian Communists, as does the emphasis on purification through labour. To be sure, hints of similar ideas can be found scattered in Lenin's writings, especially his repeated admonitions to the effect that the Party must not run too far ahead of the masses. But in fact the Bolsheviks did gallop ahead.

The essence of the concept of the mass line was codified in a resolution of the Party Central Committee dated 1 June 1943 when the Party was still in Yanan. The main principle appears in the famous slogan 'from the masses, to the masses'. This means that the Party should find out what the masses need and want, then take these 'scattered' views and bring them into systematic order. Then the task is to persuade the masses to accept this set of systematic views and 'translate them into action'. The process is, or at least then was, expected to go on over and over again. This 1943 resolution became canonical and remained in effect after the victory of 1949.[42] The immediate purpose of the resolution at the time of its adoption was to undermine the authority of Party intellectuals.[43] Mao was generally distrustful of intellectuals and often criticized them for lack of contact with the masses. Presumably he was not alone in these views. Once again we come across the notion, satirized by Bertrand Russell, of the superior virtue of the oppressed.

The source of the concept of the mass line was experience in trying to make a revolution under Chinese conditions. As early as 1925 and 1926 the Central Committee issued statements emphasizing the importance of mass support and the need 'to know and examine the opinion of the masses, which is necessary in guiding them'.[44] These statements were part of the Party's assessment of a spectacular upsurge of urban popular radicalism known as the May 30th (1925) movement. But it took a long and painful time for the Chinese Communist leadership to realize that they needed first of all an army to protect areas under their control and, of nearly equal importance, methods to gain popular support both in areas they controlled and behind enemy lines. During the late 1920s and even as late as 1938 there were frequent complaints in high Party circles about the almost total absence of mass support. But during the Communists' sojourn in Kiangsi in the early 1930s this situation changed dramatically, in response partly to recruiting on the basis of ascertained local grievances. By the early 1930s the Communists 'had organized activists among several million people in about a half-dozen areas'.[45] In Kiangsi the Chinese Communists had learned the essence of their strategic lesson and the crucial importance of the mass line. The

Yanan period was in this respect one of codification and further application.

It is clear that experience prior to taking power imparted a democratic and populist twist to Chinese Communist politics, an emphasis that appears most clearly in the theory and practice of the mass line. At this point the question that concerns us becomes: against the oppressive aspects of bureaucracy how effective a weapon has the mass line been since the Chinese communists took power? Since nearly everything that the Chinese government has done in the area of domestic politics has taken the form of a propaganda campaign, it is fair to say that the mass line has to some degree entered into almost every phase of Chinese domestic politics. Yet it is very hard to discern any sign that in practice the mass line has served as a popular check on the abuses of bureaucratic power.

For one thing, the idea of the mass line was never really intended as a check on those in authority. Instead, it represents a way of stirring up the masses to get them to do what Party leaders believe needs doing. That is the purpose of going to the masses to find out what grievances exist. I do not mean to imply that the grievances are fabricated by the Party. But it is reasonably clear that for reasons of higher politics and policies the Party selects specific grievances among a wide variety of possible ones.

The selection of grievances and objectives for mass action comes out very clearly in the case of the Great Leap Forward of 1958, which by the early 1960s had proved to be a disastrous failure. As is quite widely known, this was an attempt to achieve super-collectivization in agriculture along with great industrial growth on a local basis, the famous back-yard furnaces. There is no doubt that masses of the Chinese people drove themselves relentlessly to exhaustion and beyond in what amounted to a Chinese variant of the Russian construction of socialism in the 1930s. What is less well-known about the Great Leap Forward is its cost in human suffering. Chinese sources at the time reported no more than local areas of hunger. In 1971 a German scholar cited estimates of at least ten million deaths from famine in 1961–2. Bad weather added to mistaken policies to produce these grim results.[46] At the time ten million was regarded as an outrageous overestimate. But recently released demographic data have enabled Western scholars to compute a net loss of population during those years of at least sixteen million.[47] Presumably, as in the case of the statistics on the loss of population from Stalin's collectivization of agriculture, these sixteen million include people who were never born, due to a precipitous drop in the birth rate. Nevertheless, that total, the most conservative of the estimates made on the basis of the newly released data, is grisly enough evidence of what can happen when those in authority use all the forces at their command to pursue a disastrous policy. These figures convey a simple and important message. The Chinese variant of collectivization, for all its contact between leaders and led, Party and masses, may well have caused as much human suffering as did Stalin's brutal and authoritarian 'solution' of the Soviet Union's peasant problem. Differences of a sort there were of course. The most important one, according to an excellent comparison of the two experiences by a scholar who knows both Russian and Chinese, rests in the fact that Stalin regarded his programme as outright war against the peasants, whereas there is no evidence that Mao thought about the peasants in this way. Instead, the Great Leap Forward was a tragedy in self-deception, based on the belief that a breakthrough had occurred in agricultural production that made increased extraction of grain compatible with peasant welfare.[48] But for the peasants in Russia and China who died in these campaigns the distinction between overt policy and tragic self-deception did not make a particle of difference.

For our immediate purpose, the analysis of the mass line, it is worth noting that there may well have been some mass support for the Great Leap Forward, especially in its early stages. Most of this probably came from cadres who stirred up the peasants with visions of a happy and prosperous future after one gigantic effort. Soon, however, cadres got caught up in competitive raising of production targets by pseudo-democratic means or approval by forced acclamation. Elsewhere there are indications of passivity among the peasants. Later it came to light that numerous peasants died because local cadres prevented reports of famine from reaching Beijing.[49] As Bernstein points out, such evidence sharply contradicts the stereotype of the Maoist cadre oriented to the well-being of the masses. A problem emerges here that deserves careful investigation. Perhaps the stereotype never was all that true even in the days of Yanan. Another possibility is that a sharp transformation in the relationship between officials and ordinary citizens took place in the years following the Communist victory. Let us begin with a closer look at Mao.

Throughout most of his life Mao was trying to turn on its head the gloomy and fearful view of Gustave Le Bon (1841–1931) about the menace of the masses, though I doubt very much that he had ever heard of Le Bon. For Le Bon the masses were irrational and destructive. For Mao they were creative and, as we have seen, a source of moral purity and simplicity. Both views now look like caricatures in the light of now numerous investigations of mass and crowd behaviour.

Partly on the basis of such investigations I will now make two suggestions that may be especially helpful in understanding what follows. When accepted rules of behaviour cease to make sense and break down, for a variety of reasons that include economic hardship but are not limited to economic hardship alone, large numbers of individuals escape from social bonds and become available for movements to protest and contest the current state of affairs. There is then a lot of social tinder lying about, ready for a wide variety of purposes (though not any purpose), as Mao apparently believed in a moment of exuberance when he spoke about the people of China as a piece of blank paper.[50] Such tinder is not yet a mass that is politically useful. The Chinese Communist leaders learned this fact very painfully in the earlier stages of their movement down to the period of the Kiangsi Soviet (1931–1934). What then do the Chinese Communist leaders mean when they are talking about the masses as an active historical force? It seems to me that not only the Chinese Communists but anti-establishment radicals in general have two things in mind, of which the first is in practice by far the most important. In simple terms they mean that it is easy to get a crowd into an auditorium—or its rural equivalent —and work it up to a high level of excitement. Those who do not come to the auditorium—and these are the overwhelming majority even in periods of intense political excitement—can be labelled as politically backward. The other part of this conception of masses and mass movements holds that the leaders of the movement must have programmes and policies that will gain at least a minimum allegiance from the passive onlookers and in due course attract more active support.

This point of view helps to bring out the significance of the query that scholars sometimes put to Chinese Communist rhetoric about the masses: 'Whose masses, and who controls them?' Especially in a very fluid situation, such as the Cultural Revolution, rival leaders look for different masses to legitimate their ambitions and their policies. The rivals do not of course all start from an equal basis. Some, such as Mao himself, may be so situated in the bureaucratic structure and so surrounded by an aura of prestige—perhaps the more important factor in Mao's case—as to be nearly invulnerable. The same search for mass support goes on under relatively peaceful conditions, though in much more muted form. Just before the decision to undertake the fateful Great Leap Forward, the whole Politburo toured large parts of China. Mao was especially fond of testing what we would call grass-roots sentiment. Though MacFarquhar's instructive and detailed account of this episode has little or nothing to report on this aspect, it is plain that the whole point of the trip was to settle differences of opinion in the Politburo, cut down the opponents of 'adventurous' policies in high government offices, such as the Finance Offices, and feel out what the peasants would do if the Party leaders did take up an 'adventurous' policy. The masses are there to applaud whatever the dominant clique has decided.[51]

It is also plain that under this variant of socialism the mass of the population does not and cannot serve as much of a check on the bureaucracy or its policies even if rivals do have some sort of a popular constituency. For all their inadequacies, free elections in the liberal democracies do provide a mechanism for coping with inevitable rivalries and, on occasion, getting rid of leaders with disastrous policies.

There is one other anti-élitist device in China, the public criticism of cadres, which deserves discussion because it has had a powerful effect on the tone and character of the regime. Though this public criticism resembles the Soviet institution of self-criticism[52] I suspect that almost every Soviet bureaucrat would shudder at the thought of the strong medicine ladled out in the course of officially sponsored criticism of cadres by the Chinese masses.

From the available materials it appears that organized public criticism of cadres has been most common in the countryside. The standard objects of criticism have been basic-level cadres, that is, the lowest level of the bureaucracy and the personnel in direct contact with the peasants. The usual procedure is for the higher authorities to send down to the village a small group of reliable officers, known as a work team, to straighten out or 'rectify' village and peasant affairs.[53] One purpose in sending down a work team was to give the peasants a shield against retaliation by local cadres whom the peasants might wish to criticize. Naturally the peasants were often reluctant to speak out even against a corrupt petty tyrant on whom their fate might depend. Peasants would say 'Work teams come and go but the cadres remain. Who will protect us then?'[54] Nevertheless, after a certain amount of cajoling and reassurance by the work team some peasants did speak up. Without going into procedural details it is enough to say that a few cadres had to undergo mass 'struggle meetings' or 'organized and controlled but nevertheless extremely emotional public defamation and abuse'.[55] Suicide was a not uncommon response to such abuse.[56]

Rectification campaigns have occurred quite frequently, generally every three years or less,[57] though not necessarily with public humiliation of cadres each time. The one that followed the failure of the Great Leap Forward, and was part of the Socialist Education Movement of 1962–5, appears to have been especially severe. At points especially selected as targets for work teams, some 60 per cent or more of all local cadres were subjected to criticism that often involved struggle and public humiliation.[58] This type of behaviour appeared again in the Cultural Revolution at its height during 1966 and 1967. That was a violent explosion against almost all forms of authority. In contrast to the campaigns discussed above the Cultural Revolution was mainly an affair of the cities. The targets were also much more highly placed. Some of its publicly humiliated victims were near the apex of the regime. And at least some of the militants expressed frustration at the limitations of the Cultural Revolution because the movement held back from a structural solution of China's political problems. Some militants even went so far as to describe Mao's 'extensive concessions to the bourgeoisie', in the form of high salaries and special privileges for high officials, as a 'pure expression' of the forces they sought to overcome.[59]

The attacks on local cadres began shortly after the establishment of the new regime and uncovered some abuses. But they have also demoralized local cadres on a very wide scale. The position of a local cadre is in any case exposed and difficult. Such an official stands between the irresistable force of Party pressures and the immovable object of local habits, customs, and personal connection. To reach a *modus vivendi* with both worlds is far from easy. The Party line of today may become the deviation of tomorrow, as has so often happened in the past. Lower ranking cadres frequently get the blame for whatever goes wrong with the leaders' policy. Hence for a cadre the wisest course of action may be to limit one's zeal for the revolutionary cause to purely verbal incantations. In this way the Party's main instruments for the execution of policy lose their edge and become corroded.

Public criticism of cadres has provided ordinary citizens with an opportunity to fight back at the bureaucracy and to correct abuses. However, up until the Cultural Revolution the Party carefully selected the abuses and the human targets for public criticism. In other words, the Party made the basic decisions about what people could complain about. For this and other reasons ordinary citizens might display a disturbing lack of spontaneous enthusiasm for organized public criticism.[60] During the Cultural Revolution the Party's control over public criticism temporarily broke down, mainly because Mao wanted to break the back of the Party bureaucracy. But this anarchic situation was hardly conducive to what we might call freedom of complaint. A semi-spontaneous radical tornado swept over large parts of China. People who could not bend with the wind like grass or were caught in an exposed position found themselves swept toward destruction. If there are limitations on the opportunity to express grievances in public criticism, there are evidently at least equal limitations on the effectiveness of this device in rooting out abuses. All the old ones remain, according to current complaints and reports. The main effect, as mentioned above, has been to paralyze the lower ranking cadres.

It has often been said that Mao unlike Stalin did not resort to killing his opponents. That appears to be only a partial truth. In 1930 he suppressed a military rebellion in what became known as the Fut'ien incident. His opponents in the Party accused him of widespread executions and indiscriminate use of torture. Though the accusations are undoubtedly exaggerated and the incident obscure, it does seem reasonably plain that Mao—and other leaders at this time—did resort to killing their opponents.[61] Even if we set aside this partial limitation on Mao's alleged lack of cruelty, a troubling question remains. How much worse is death by execution than public humiliation that can drive a person to suicide?

Since so many of the present leaders of China have returned to power after various forms of disgrace, it is obvious how they would answer the question. But it seems likely that their own experiences combined with a political need to restore order made them decide to put public criticism of cadres on the shelf. Mao left this earth to go talk with Marx, as he often put it, in 1976. In 1977 his successors moved gingerly to eliminate the disciplinary role of the masses, though the masses were still to 'help keep the Party on its toes'. There was to be a return to the traditional mass line form of popular participation. What the leaders apparently wanted was mobilized yet orderly masses.[62]

That, of course, is the dream of every twentieth-century political leader in every kind of political regime. Unlike other dreams this one has come true only too often for the ones with repressive objectives.

7 Inequality and authority after Mao

Because the changes in official policy since Mao's death in 1976 shed a revealing light backward on Maoist attempts to transform Chinese society, it will be useful to close with a brief review of these changes. Their main thrust has been to dismount what there was in the way of egalitarian–communitarian socialism and replace it with a meritocratic socialism that includes capitalist features. In more concrete terms the government has been trying to establish a much closer connection between effort, ability, and material rewards. The main reason appears to be that egalitarianism, together with the absence of a visible connection between effort and reward, have prevented badly needed increases in the productivity of both industry and agriculture. This threat to productivity is not merely a matter of Chinese national pride or whether China will some day become a modern industrial power. It is also a question of whether the Chinese will ever have enough to eat.

The journey toward meritocracy and away from socialist purity, which promises to be a very long journey, has already displayed twists and turns, as well as temporary reversals of direction. These twistings about reflect not only vested socialist interests in incompetence but also genuine crises of conscience. It seems that these crises occur throughout the society, from the poorest peasants up through committed cadres all the way to the real rulers of China in the top Party élite, where it is clear there have been stormy debates. 'Why did we give the best part of our lives to the fight for Communism', they seem to be saying, 'if the government wants to restore capitalism?' The most important, or at least the most visible, of these attempts to restore socialist purity was the Campaign against Spiritual Pollution. The pollution supposedly came from the Western bourgeoisie (more specifically Hong Kong) and took the form of clothes, popular music, sunglasses, etc., all with an erotic tinge. (It is interesting that socialist youth in China, as in Russia, whenever it gets a chance, stampedes in search of the trashiest elements of Western culture.) The Campaign against Spiritual Pollution was thus a reassertion of socialist morality in its more puritanical version. It began in September 1983 and ended only six months later. The end is revealing. The top Party leadership became unenthusiastic about the campaign because it was distracting attention from Party rectification and economic work. Therefore they issued a decree asserting that pollution was not to be found in the countryside, the factories, or the natural sciences. In other words, it did not exist.[63] Hardly a great event in its own right, the fate of the Campaign against Spiritual Pollution reveals how swiftly major policies and the political atmosphere of daily life can change.

The changes in agricultural policy and organization have so far been the most far-reaching and startling. They began in 1978 with the first increase in twelve years of state procurement prices for major farm products. By 1981 these prices, paid to collective farms for compulsory deliveries as in the Soviet Union, had risen by an average of 42 per cent over the level of 1977.[64] But apparently the authorities concluded that merely increasing the financial rewards was not enough and that a thorough reorganization was necessary. In 1979 they introduced what is known as the 'responsibility system' and by 1981 managed to get it adopted in more than 80 per cent of China's agricultural units.[65] Under the new system individual households take responsibility for growing a certain amount of produce. Formerly this responsibility or obligation rested on the production teams, which have now, in some areas at least, broken up for lack of anything to do. By the new system, peasant families plant and work separate fields and profit separately from their own crop yields. Most of the collective property in tools has been distributed to individual families. By 1982, according to one excellent account of a village near Canton, the village's fields had become tantamount to private landholdings, since the allocation of land was on a semi-permanent basis.[66]

If official statistics are to be trusted, the government's new policies have produced a remarkable improvement in the peasants' material situation. A nationwide sampling of peasant incomes in 1978 found that poor peasant families with an annual income of less than 150 yuan per person came to 65 per cent of the sample. In 1983 the proportion of the poor fell to 7.6 per cent. The more prosperous families with an annual income of over 300 yuan per person made up only 2.4 per cent of the sample in 1978, but by 1983 the proportion of the well-to-do rose to 46.4 per cent.[67] These figures seem too good to be true. They recall the exaggerated claims made for the opposite kinds of policies under the Great Leap Forward.

A study of peasant incomes in the province of Heilongjiang in Northern Manchuria, published in August 1985, gives a much more sombre picture. Though the evidence refers to only one province in the far North where agriculture faces special difficulties, it is likely that the situation there is echoed in other areas. The study divides peasant incomes into three grades. The first one consists of the well-to-do with annual incomes per capita of over 500 yuan. These households have plenty of workers, more land than the others, good mechnical equipment (including tractors in some cases), and sources of outside income. But the well-to-do make up only 18 per cent of the rural population. The second category with incomes per capita between 200 and 500 yuan includes those who just get by with enough for food and clothing. They lack the advantages of the first group, especially outside income. With surprising candour the report states that the households in this category are dangerously exposed not only to the vagaries of the weather and natural disasters but also to changes in agricultural policy. They work and live at a level of subsistence and play no part in market relationships. Yet this second group is the largest of all, making up about 60 per cent of the rural households. Beneath them are the poor, or those persons with incomes beneath the subsistence level of 200 yuan annually. They make up more than a fifth or 21 per cent of the rural households. Many of these do not have enough to eat and require some form of government assistance, such as extra grain, just to survive. Thus the poor and those who just squeak by make up 80 per cent of the rural population in this northern area.[68]

From this report and other evidence the impression emerges that the government's new agrarian policies have helped to generate a substantial upper level of prosperous peasants. After all, a fifth would be a noteworthy proportion. It also seems likely that peasants lower down the income scale have made some gains. Yet it seems that a large mass of the peasantry in the area studied still leads a precarious existence in what Westerners would regard as grinding poverty.

The government's agrarian policy amounts to a partial dismantling of socialism and a partial return to private property in farming. The transformation is important enough to explode widespread Western notions about socialism being the inevitable next stage of human history. Even such a familiar phrase as 'late monopoly capitalism' with its implication that socialism will soon replace a faltering capitalism, becomes nonsensical when we can see socialism turning into capitalism under our own eyes. Nevertheless, there are certain qualifications and limitations to this transformation that we have to perceive in order to appraise it correctly. The peasant's 'private property' exists still within a bureaucratic socialist framework that sets production targets, prices, taxes, and controls the supply of inputs into agriculture, such as fertilizer.[69] Production teams seem to be necessary for this bureaucratic machinery to work, and one wonders what will happen if they wither away on a wide scale.

In the second place, by no means are all peasants enthusiastic about the new capitalism. Some regret the way the old production teams guaranteed a minimum of food in case of extreme poverty and can see that some undertakings, like improvements in irrigation, impose demands for labour and materials far beyond the capabilities of individual households.[70] Finally, it is well to remember that this is not the first case of a socialist regime's return toward capitalism. When the Soviet Union adopted the New Economic Policy in 1921 there were those who thought that socialism was finished because it had already demonstrated its inherent failures. Instead, as we know, socialism went on to greater and bloodier triumphs.

In turning from changes in rural policy to those affecting the urban population, especially the workers, one realizes that the fundamental inequality in Chinese society has for some time been that between the urban and the rural inhabitants. The city dwellers, only about one-fifth of the total population, have come to form a relatively prosperous and protected enclave. In 1958 the government passed a series of tough laws to stop rural migration into the cities. The Chinese Communists did this to prevent the emergence of standard urban social pathologies such as a crime-prone slum population. On this score they have been quite successful, though in recent years educated and jobless youth has furnished another social base for criminal activity.

The prohibition on moving to the city works through denying ration cards to illegal immigrants. Without the shortages that make ration cards necessary the prohibition would be unenforceable. This situation strengthens the thesis that shortages of material goods are necessary to make socialism work and that under socialism the power to ration is the power to rule. Socialist governments do not sit on bayonets so much as on ration books. Socialist politicians probably do not say as much even to themselves. But that is what their propaganda about sacrifices for building socialism turns out to mean in practice.

Meanwhile government policies and prevailing circumstances have produced a protective wall around the urban workers, at least those in state-run enterprises, to shield them against many of the vicissitudes of economic life. The most important of these was *de facto* permanent employment, known as 'the iron rice bowl'.[71] If wages seemed low and were kept down by government decree,[72] nevertheless they constituted a regular and predictable source of income. This the peasants lacked, since the ordinary peasant depended on the fluctuating value of workpoints on his particular farm. In addition, the city workers in state-run firms had at their disposal a set of medical services for minimal fees. Finally, there were pensions, disability benefits, and a variety of other social programmes.[73] In the 1970s, it is claimed, the funds set aside for welfare benefits amounted to 17 per cent of the wage bill.[74]

According to careful and objective Western scholars, there were some heavy costs to this programme of protecting the workers. In the course of time the egalitarian incomes policy, the official wage freeze, and high job security generated absenteeism, shoddy work, and sheer laziness on a wide scale.[75] So far the government's response to this form of behaviour has been cautious. Nor is this caution surprising. Urban workers resemble a praetorian guard for socialism, and it is risky to discipline the praetorian guard. Still the government has done something. It has addressed the issue of the workers' motivation by increasing material incentives, encouraging piece rates and cash bonuses. It has also encouraged the authorities in some work units to 'break the "iron rice bowl"' by discharging employees who create serious problems in the shop.[76]

The government has also tackled the problem of an industrial management stifled by its bureaucratic environment or content to rest on its oars while making the correct political noises in time with the ever shifting forms of Party indignation. Since 1981 there have been experiments linking rewards to the profits earned by each enterprise, a long established practice in the USSR. More recently there has been an effort to get the Chinese manager to emulate the capitalist entre-preneurs by replacing the 'big pot' system of egalitarian wages with wages tied to output and by using Japanese methods of building community spirit in the factory. More important is the practice of contracting out, as in agriculture, small and medium sized enterprises to individuals and collectives. That means greater autonomy *and* responsibility for the individual manager. He has to scare up the necessary raw materials on his own, keep the workers reasonably happy and working effectively, and turn out useful products of satisfactory quality. None of that is easy in any society.[77]

On October 20, 1984 the Party Central Committee issued a major statement on economic policy for the foreseeable future that codified these practices and announced other policies of the same type. The main thrust of these measures is to introduce a series of capitalist practices in order to make socialism work and raise the standard of living. For the time being at least there is to be no more talk about the superior virtues of the poor and the transformation of human nature by communal living. The capitalist practices include inequalities in income as an incentive to work, freeing plant managers from political superivision, and most important of all the widespread introduction of the market as the device that regulates the economy. Many—perhaps most—plant managers will have to cover the costs of production in turning out goods that will sell at a price customers will be willing to pay. Such measures imply, as the Party recognizes, an overhaul of the existing price system, in which prices frequently fail to reflect either costs of production or effective demand.

Two major socialist safeguards form part of the new economic order. Certain industrial products of national importance—coal, oil, steel, and cigarettes are among them—remain subject to the command economy of compulsory plans and quotas for delivery. Plant autonomy in the form just described is supposed to go into effect in the next lower tier of the economy: the large and medium sized urban plants. There are more than a million of these that employ more than 80 million manual and clerical workers. But this autonomy has strict limits since the government will continue to regulate prices. Autonomy is supposed to exist within limits set by the government. In addition, the manager's authority is to be limited by elected representatives of the workers and clerical personnel, because, says the Party decision, the plant will be a modern socialist plant. This limit, of course, exists in liberal capitalist plants too, and it remains to be seen what powers these elected representatives will have in practice. Hence, as one looks more closely at the details, it becomes apparent that the Chinese variant of the New Economic Policy could develop in either of two directions. The market could assume major importance, or the situation could remain pretty much the same as it has been. According to present plans the market will be allowed full play only for certain agricultural products and the vital service sector, where as of 1983 there were already more than 5 million private households engaged in economic activities.[78]

To repeat, then, meritocracy, in the sense of being able to turn out the goods, has become the order of the day in industry as well as agriculture. That, at least, is the official rhetoric. Whether the government can really introduce meritocracy in opposition to entrenched socialist practices, as well as those inherited from the Chinese imperial past, and make it the essential basis of the social order remains to be seen. I doubt that this can happen in China or anywhere else for that matter. Nowhere to my knowledge do human beings like to be tested for competence, especially not at frequent intervals. Everywhere we see that a great deal of the resistance to industrialization has been resistance to the demands for new forms of competence. At all levels of the social order and in all societies that have faced these demands, human beings have shown themselves adept at evading the requirements for competence and clothing their evasion with assorted garments of ethical principle.

The urban school system is the social sector where the repudiation of egalitarianism and the attempt to establish a meritocracy are most visible. Equal access to neighbourhood schools has given way to a hierarchy of schools of varying quality. Acceptance as a student in a good school depends primarily on scores in entrance examinations. At the secondary level, a series of 'keypoint schools' receives the most resources, the best teachers, and as students the top performers in examinations. Christopher Jencks, as mentioned in the first chapter, tells us that in the United States all these measures are pretty much a waste of time. It would be interesting to know whether this kind of meritocratic policy is equally futile in China. I suspect not. The current Chinese assumption is that higher education imparts knowledge and skills useful for policy-making. It seems to me that higher education is more likely to create and hone skills useful for medium-grade administration than for getting to the top rungs of the political ladder. In any case, the successors to Mao have put all their chips on educational inequality. The content of the schooling would cheer the most conservative Western pedagogue. Politics and education through labour have been cut back substantially. The emphasis is on academics again 'with a vengeance'. Strict tests and grading are once more in vogue, with the authority of the teacher restored. Those who do best in entrance examinations can now proceed directly to a university without any intervening stint of labour in the countryside.[79]

The conservative restoration in the educational system can succeed only if the youngsters—or at least a good many youngsters—can find an acceptable job on completing their education. Otherwise, if the effort does not pay off in a way they regard as satisfactory, many will

cease to accept the whole ethic of hard work and turn to forms of
political and cultural deviance. A juvenile gang subculture and models
of political and cultural deviance have already been well established.
So far Chinese socialism has not found a solution to the overproduc-
tion of middle-school graduates.[80] But China might just possibly be on
the way toward a solution. One straw in the wind is the announcement
on 1 June 1985 of government plans to increase the proportion of
vocational graduates from secondary schools from the current level of
32 per cent to 50 per cent by 1990.[81]

For a bit more solid information let us glance briefly at the state of
unemployment. According to Chinese sources in 1979, some five to
eleven per cent of the non-agricultural labour force were unemployed,
figures that are on the high side. Three years later, by the beginning of
1982 the figure was reported to be down to three per cent.[82] On the
other hand, it is by no means clear that this reduction in urban
unemployment will reduce suspicion of work and education. A considerable number of the unemployed seems to have been absorbed by
reducing the investment in capital-intensive state industry and increasing funds for collective enterprises with low earnings and few fringe
benefits, like bicycle repair shops and other services that are labour-
intensive. Now it is reasonably plain that youngsters will not compete
in school in order to work in a bicycle repair shop, but that they might
wish to get more schooling to become plant managers or get a job in
one of the ministries. Hence we cannot be sure that the policy of
encouraging small-scale enterprises will accomplish much toward
making an education seem worthwhile. It is all very well in the West to
say that a good education is a value in its own right, as I believe very
firmly. On the other hand, without some support in income and
status—or the sense that one is doing something worthwhile that
enables one to eat regularly—an education can merely turn the world
sour and lead to behaviour destructive for oneself and others. Only the
future will show whether Chinese socialism can cope with this
problem.

To put this issue in a wider setting, so far the Chinese and Russian
evidence suggests that decay in socialist systems proceeds from the top
down, as it has in preceding forms of civilization. A very small amount
of force can keep the expression of a large amount of popular discontent within bounds tolerable to the rulers. Disintegration begins when
the rulers start to quarrel among themselves about the premises of the

social order, the bases of their legitimacy and authority. In both China and Russia these disputes are visible just below the surface of official unity of doctrine and policy. As long as the disputes can be contained or resolved—by force if necessary—these regimes can survive and adapt to new circumstances.

5

IMPLICATIONS

1 *Comparative observations*

Up to this point our task has been to explain as best we can the systems of authority and inequality in three quite different societies. In bringing this work to a close I shall try to provide explicit answers to questions inherent in the undertaking itself and that have, in all likelihood, arisen in the minds of my readers. What, after all, are the significant similarities and differences among these three societies? To put the question slightly differently, in what ways does socialism differ from capitalism and what major differences and similarities do we see among the dominant states in the socialist camp? Then what larger meaning, if any, is there to the body of facts or alleged facts presented and interpreted in this study? Can we set this evidence in a meaningful way in a framework of larger world-wide political trends? That I shall try to do shortly. First it is necessary to discuss similarities and differences in a brief comparative analysis.

It is impossible to reach a satisfactory result by taking each case separately, analyzing it, and then comparing the results, even though a separate analysis of each case provides indispensable information. The reason why this caricature of analytical methods in the natural sciences will not work here is the existence of an historical relationship between these three societies and their predecessors. This relationship goes a long way toward providing an explanation of the character of authority and inequality in each of the three societies. Each society was reacting against its historical predecessor, trying to improve on it by avoiding or reducing earlier forms of unjust authority and inequality. (There is perhaps a hint of the Hegelian dialectic in such changes.)

The United States came into existence against the European system of more or less absolute monarchy and hereditary nobility. This impetus is still visible today in the marked hostility toward hereditary or unearned privilege and eminence, together with a noticeable current of suspicion even about forms of eminence that have ostensibly been earned, such as leadership in science and the arts. Achieved eminence in these fields can suggest the existence of limits to the wisdom of the common man, generally an unpalatable suggestion in the United States. To the extent that a person becomes a leader in the arts and sciences, that person ceases to be a common man or woman. This is not true, however, of leading figures in sports and entertainment. Such figures Americans take to their hearts without reservation, raising no objections to their frequently astronomical earnings (or known addictions to alcohol or drugs, if these habits do not affect their performances). Entertainers and heroes of sport are seen as superior without being threatening since their chief function is to entertain. Indeed, they often become models to the young, frequently with parental approval. But when current figures lose leading qualities as entertainers, the public can easily cast them aside and replace them with new models.

More importantly the streak of hostility to rules and restraints so marked in the United States had its roots in the American reaction over two centuries ago against allegedly arbitrary royal authority. Originally bolstered by opportunities for personal enrichment in a new land, Americans still defend the right of an individual to do what he or she wants to do or has been used to doing. 'It's a free country', they vehemently assert. The burden of proof is on the government, federal or local, to prove that a given form of behaviour actually is socially dangerous and harmful. Even if that proof has passed into law, many individuals refuse to change their behaviour, claiming that it is up to the government to catch them if they stick to their familiar habits.

Many Americans today vehemently resist having 'the law' tell them what is good for them. At the same time there are an enormous number of laws on American statute books that do just that. The reason for this contradiction is, I suspect, the absence of a clear consensus about what the law should do or even about an appropriate set of goals for their own society more specific than the most general platitudes about freedom. Hence a multitude of special-interest groups pushes hard, each for its pet legislation. For legislators high and low it is easiest to give in to this clamour, and thus to silence it. Some socially desirable legislation, such as the Social Security Act, has come into existence this way. But a major result is to load up the statute books with contradictory and unenforceable laws and ordinances. In turn the result of this situation is to increase the general public's disrespect for law and authority even further.

Just as the United States came into existence as a reaction against royal absolutism and hereditary privilege, a reaction that in time would create the purest form of capitalism, so the Soviet Union, as the first socialist state, came into existence as a negative and hostile reaction to capitalism. Lenin's conception of capitalism was not, of course, based on the North American model alone. It included also England, France, and Germany. Lenin seems to have regarded the United States as less evil or at any rate less relevant to European affairs. After the seizure of power he was uncritically eager to borrow American theories of business management (e.g., Taylorism) and American technological expertise in order to set up a workable socialism in Russia. Because of this ambivalence toward American capitalism and because Lenin spent most of his energy attacking potential rivals on the left and arguing for his own versions of a grand revolutionary strategy, it is not easy to determine just what his grievances against capitalism were. Both he and his Russian Marxist rivals seem to have taken these grievances for granted as something that intelligent and busy people did not have to discuss. The job now, it may have seemed to them, especially in the midst of the First World War, was to get rid of capitalism as fast as possible, not to argue about its evils.

The war suffused Marxist thinking of the time, and, of course, not only Marxist. Lenin was as horrified as anyone at the apparently senseless slaughter. In the theory of imperialism, to which he made a contribution more famous than distinguished, Lenin believed that he had at hand both a diagnosis and a remedy for all the senseless carnage. Imperialist rivalries were the cause of wars in modern industrial societies. Capitalism would collapse without the extra profits to be had in exploiting economically backward areas. The remedy flowed obviously from the diagnosis: the abolition of capitalism and its replacement by socialism would end the exploitation and rivalries that fed modern wars. Just how and why socialism would end these rivalries Lenin never paused to make clear.

Even if the leaders of the first socialist state came to power on an anti-capitalist programme, these leaders wanted or felt they had to have some of the major creations of capitalism, and above all big industry. Stalin gave Russia just that through four interrelated policies: (1) the war against the peasant in the form of forced collectivization of agriculture, (2) forced draft industrialization, (3) a flat rejection of 'equality mongering' in pay scales, and (4) widespread arbitrary terror. Stalin's policy of paying one man more and shooting the others did get results, though it would be hard to maintain that it was the most effective way to industrialize rapidly.

The Chinese Communists rose to power against the alleged and obvious abuses of a decaying political order into which European powers were intruding like vultures waiting for the death rattle. At the same time it is easy to discern, especially in the policies and pro-nouncements of Mao, a rejection—though not complete—of Leninist strategies for gaining power and creating a new social order. Much of the rejection is traceable to the circumstances of the Chinese Com-munist rise to power. As a revolutionary party that had finally learned how to attract peasant support, the Chinese Communists were less likely than the Bolsheviks to declare war on the peasants. On the other hand, this factor did not prevent the Chinese Communists from doing great damage to the peasants in that burst of enthusiastic self-deception that became known as the Great Leap Forward. The Maoist reluctance to shoot colleagues and subordinates likewise stems at least partly from the fact that much of Mao's prestige came from his having been in earlier days a victim of Party intrigues. Comradely socialist equality was also an adaptation to the Spartan conditions of guerrilla warfare. It was not likely to withstand the requirements of managing a huge, varied, and very civilized society.

To replace the autocratic methods of a Stalin, Mao and at least some of his associates hoped to be able to rely on revolutionary enthusiasm based on an egalitarian and co-operative ethic. This sub-stitution does not appear to have taken much effect in practice nor to have had desirable results where it did take effect. So far as I can make out, it was mainly useful as a club to beat the Russians over the head with charges of revisionism and thereby certify the doctrinal purity of the Chinese road to socialism. The most noticeable impact of the egalitarian and co-operative ethic occurred during the Cultural Revo-lution. Probably that was not quite as much of a disaster as the current Chinese leadership would like us to believe. But it hardly helped the economy and certainly produced widespread moral confusion and disillusionment. Since the defeat of the radical Maoist forces following the death of their leader, the government has been replacing the revolutionary egalitarian and co-operative ethic with a meritocratic one, while trying to keep this new individualism under control by drawing on suitable fragments from older revolutionary doctrines. It is not an easy balancing act.

In the course of its development Chinese Communist theory and practice have displayed several features that distinguish them from their counterpart in the USSR. The most striking is the use of the small group as a device for the indoctrination and control of the population. It is not clear, on the other hand, what has happened to this device since Mao's death. Its heavy emphasis on getting the proper attitude and theoretical outlook is out of tune with Deng's *enrichissez-vous* variant of socialism. Another distinctive feature is the mass line, even if here practice is rather far from theory. Still another element is the general atmosphere of hostility to bureaucracy promoted by Mao. It is true that both the Russian and the Chinese leaders use and encourage popular hostility toward officialdom in order to control bureaucrats. But Stalin shot bureaucrats whereas Mao turned popular fury (much of it no doubt artificially stimulated) against them in the Cultural Revolution. Both the Stalinist Terror and the Cultural Revolution were the sort of exaggerated events that reveal essential elements in the so-called normal functioning of a political system. Finally, China stands out for having dismounted collective agriculture. It is important to recall, however, that the individual peasant still works within a socialist framework.

The main similarities between the two socialist giants are familiar enough to require no more than a brief listing. They include (1) a one-party state that attempts to enforce its version of doctrinal orthodoxy on the population at large; (2) a powerful and omnipresent secret police; (3) bureaucratic central control of large sectors of the economy (a system which by now has generated enough dissatisfaction to produce attempts at simplification and improvement); and (4) corruption that appears to be on the increase. These shared traits do not of course correspond with the earlier idealistic intentions of the revolutionary founders. The distinctive traits of both systems are traceable to the specific historical conditions in which their revolutions occurred, as well as their pre-revolutionary culture and social structure. In terms of the number of people they affect and the depth of their impact, the socialist and shared traits are far more powerful than the historically specific ones, Russian or Chinese. Indeed the separation is artificial. There is, for example, in the case of the Cultural Revolution, a specifically Chinese and Maoist way of responding to a situation created by a revolutionary take-over.

If revolutionary socialism is what counts in the USSR and China, we can see a roughly similar situation among the societies in the liberal capitalist camp. Certainly the United States differs from England, France, West Germany, and other countries with a democratic form of government and an advanced economy. But even in the case of West

Germany, where political democracy was the product of defeat in the Second World War, one could maintain that industrialization and political democracy affect the life of the people more deeply than the historical legacy of Frederick the Great and Bismarck.

But let us look more closely at capitalism and socialism. When we observe their systems of authority there are three similarities that stand out. They are (1) a shared reluctance to accept hierarchy, that is, the necessity for command–obedience relationships in order to co-ordi-nate the varied activities of the state as a whole and the various groups within it; (2) a corresponding reluctance to accept the notion of inevitable conflicts of interest among different social groups; and (3) a reluctance to accept the social inequalities deriving from hierarchy and group conflict in which some sectors of the population are bound to be losers. The conflict between this generalized reluctance and the his-torically specific pressures for the acceptance of hierarchy, group conflict, and social inequality has had quite different outcomes in each case.

Though the United States displays a strong antinomian or rebellious current throughout its history, much of this is rhetoric that has not prevented American citizens from coming to terms with authority whenever political or economic forces seemed to make it necessary. We seem to be a nation of grumbling conformists. That may be partly due to the partial acceptance of group conflict at a relatively early date in our history. Like the English, the inhabitants of the United States developed to a high degree the theory and practice of a legitimate opposition, something that never took root in Russian or Chinese socialism despite all the talk about democratic centralism. Legitimate opposition implies the right to select serious issues and complain about them in a way that embarrasses those in authority. There is also of course a great deal of public complaint in socialist societies, but there the higher authority selects the targets in accord with current policy. Under socialism, unauthorized complaint smacks of faction and sub-version. Chronic crises and permanent mobilization in socialist societies have stifled the development of Western forms of legitimate opposition. The stifling took place in societies where pre-industrial social and cultural trends had already been unfavourable to liberal capitalist development. Nevertheless, we must avoid writing victors' history by overlooking the indigenous seeds of liberal authority that did sprout in these societies before the revolutions.

To return to current issues, Stalin, as we have seen, did come to terms with the need for hierarchy and even did so with a vengeance. Yet there remain signs of a guilty conscience about all this. The Soviet élite cannot enjoy many of its privileges openly. What can be purchased in special stores is not public knowledge the way it is in the West. Nor is it widely known who lives in which fancy *dacha* and at what level of abundance.

To be sure, Mao, whose opposition to hierarchy and social inequality was the strongest, did on occasion talk about conflict among groups as something that would last indefinitely under socialism. For him there were two kinds of group conflict. One was disputes within the socialist camp that were to be handled by persuasion. The other was the conflict between socialists and anti-socialists that in the end could only be settled by force. One can discern in the settlement of disputes among socialists by persuasion the germ of a system of legitimate opposition. But the situation did not work out that way, partly because it was temptingly easy to pin the label of 'fake socialist' or 'capitalist roader' on nearly any distinguished leader who opposed one's policies. By pinning the label of capitalist roader on an opponent one ruled him out of the group of 'real' socialists and put him in the camp of the enemy, against whom all weapons were acceptable. Hence politics remained at the level of savage factional conflict.

To avoid misunderstanding and to put these observations in perspective it will be helpful to make some general comments on the limits of social criticism and the way these limits work in other societies. There is no such thing as a society without limits about what one can say about other individuals or groups. At the outer edge of these limits are those set by culture, which prevent people from even thinking certain types of thoughts. We might say, for example, that the notion of a secret police probably could not occur to the Eskimos before contact with the whites. Usually the limits are much narrower and prevent or try to prevent the expression of ideas that are quite thinkable but deemed socially dangerous. In a complex society with a written language these limits can vary a great deal from one social class to another and even groups and institutions within social classes. In even the most perfect tyranny there are likely to be noticeable variations in what can be said and where. Unless the dictator is able to make all decisions himself—a rare and unlikely prospect—there will have to be meetings of the top leaders to discuss major issues of political and economic strategy. The less certain the dictator feels about the probable outcome of different strategies—often enough all options may seem threatening—the more room there will be for impassioned debate. Hence, even in a perfect or nearly perfect tyranny, there can be a crucial area of free speech. There can even be strong pressure for several such areas if the need for open and informed discussion arises at other strategic points in the social order. Research in the natural sciences and the advantages of objective military and political intelligence are familiar examples.

Under liberal capitalism the limitations take a different form. In the United States it is possible to say just about anything without going to gaol or getting shot, though if one wants to put highly seasoned remarks in print in a major newspaper or other public medium one has to take account of laws about libel. But at any given point in time what one says has little or no effect if it is outside the mainstream of accepted public discourse. This mainstream constitutes a narrow band of acceptable and 'responsible' ideas in the wider spectrum of possible and worthwhile ideas. All this is likely to be familiar enough to any detached observer of the American scene. The puzzling and interesting point remains: how does the content of the mainstream change over time? What makes the range of socially acceptable intellectual options expand or contract? Simply on the basis of having lived through numerous expansions and contractions I would suggest that articulate spokesmen for ideas and practices on the right or the left of respectable opinion can and do change the character and content of this opinion, especially when their arguments seem to explain current events or suggest a way to cope with these events.

As we turn from aspects of authority to those of inequality the picture that first comes into view is this: in the two leading socialist societies the Communist Party has invested a large but decreasing amount of energy in the effort to remake human society—and through the society human beings themselves—in accord with the goal of a classless society. Liberal capitalist society, despite a substantial egalitarian element in its formal doctrine, operates on a different principle. From its early phase at the time of Adam Smith, the liberal capitalist outlook has accepted human nature as it had been formed by the historical forces of early capitalism. The image of human nature thus perceived was not very flattering. It included strong traits of greed and selfishness along with an individualism that was almost anti-social. But—and this was the main point—liberal capitalists, or their more influential spokesmen, expected the market to transmute these unlovely traits into socially constructive behaviour and results, such as more and better quality food for the masses, more comfortable and better housing, etc., etc.[1] As these promises came true and industrial giants emerged to meet old human needs and create new ones, the role of the market diminished. With this dimunition there was a loss in society's power to transmute anti-social traits into socially constructive ones. (Perhaps there has been less of this social alchemy anyway than some of us were inclined to believe.) In any case, liberal capitalist regimes, by refusing to give much more than lip service to human equality, managed to create a prosperity. But they are now in obvious trouble at the hands of those who feel excluded from the prosperity.

Meanwhile the socialists started from the opposite premise that the market was the main source of all that was evil and unjust in modern capitalist society. Hence they came close to exterminating the market in their versions of socialism. They are by now stuck with social systems that work at least as badly as advanced capitalism and for some of the same reasons.[2] On this account they have been experimenting with the market to see if it cannot produce constructive results for them too. Both socialist and conservative governments have been turning to the market as a remedy for their distress. It appears that they have tried everything else, and nothing has worked. There are reasons to doubt that the market will work either. There may be a symptom of political bankruptcy in all this, an issue I would prefer to postpone with the observation that supposedly bankrupt societies often last a very long time. At this point, instead, we should look more closely at the sources of inequality and justifications for it in the United States, the USSR, and China.

Under capitalism, opportunities for private individuals to gain control of major resources, as for example in mining and transportation, for both of which there came to be a very large demand, provided the basis for huge fortunes. It was not so much the making of a better mousetrap that counted as getting control of mousetrap-making. At lower levels of the income pyramid it has been mainly skill that has counted. Again this means skill for which there is a social demand. An electronics technician can command forty to sixty dollars an hour depending on location, not all of which to be sure will go into the technician's pocket. A poet with an excellent command of the technique of writing sonnets cannot make a living. By and large it seems from the evidence of polls and interviews that the American population is on the whole quite well satisfied with this situation. Its strongest justification is that it needs no justification. To be sure, a good many

Americans will assert that a few people at the top of the income pyramid get too much and quite a few more at the bottom get too little. An occasional iconoclast will raise questions about how good an index to human worth a large income might be. For all these reservations and quibbles the citizens of the United States seem quite well satisfied with their system of social inequality. Race and ethnic differences present the only flaw, and a serious one. However, large numbers of people can pass their whole lives without encountering racial or ethnic issues. As for the general satisfaction with the American way of inequality, it is hardly surprising—or revolting—unless one looks at the United States from the standpoint of a strong egalitarian commitment. The American system of inequality is one that Americans have created by themselves for themselves. It is not the product of an alien philosophical creed. Nor does it contain the relics of a pre-capitalist system of inequality that at times make European systems of inequality full of anachronisms that charm but also irritate.

For comparative purposes it is important to add that under the liberal capitalist system there are many different ladders leading to different degrees of success and esteem, even if the influence of money exerts strong pressure toward creating a single ladder. Furthermore, for all the talk about big corporations really running America, not even the most powerful corporation executive in the country, or its richest citizen, can by his or her decisions have an impact on a fraction of the lives of ordinary people affected by a decision of a top official in a socialist country.

In the Soviet Union and China it is almost impossible for an individual to appropriate permanently either resources or social functions. To be sure, Stalin and Mao managed to keep control over major aspects of policy-making for their whole lives. But they had to fight to keep their positions, and their power to determine policy was at times quite limited. There are also a good many officials, especially in China, who have managed to get something like seniority rights to their positions. Yet none of these exceptions, important though they are, match the security of property rights backed up by the full power of the law and considerable popular sentiment in a liberal capitalist regime. In the absence of such property rights under socialism, the only route to status and access to the material bases of civilized existence lies through the bureaucracy. Other ladders to success, such as the arts and sciences, are rudimentary and subject to being kicked out from under the climbers by Party officials. For the socialist individual the situation requires making the right noises at the right time and avoiding the wrong noises. There is not much room in this system for the self-defined genius or the real one who in a liberal capitalist society gets stored in a committee or a research foundation, just in case his or her ideas might come in handy some day. That is not simply because socialist bureaucracies are still relatively poor. They are also scared of unorthodoxy as well as never quite sure what is or will be unorthodox. With other routes to security and esteem closed off, bureaucracy remains a limited substitute because status goes with the bureaucratic slot, not with the human being who happens to fill the slot. The human being who loses the slot loses the prerequisites and the esteem, indeed everything. He does not have the prestige of being, let us say, former chief assistant to X or Y. Instead, he or she is likely to be under a cloud for having lost a job. Meanwhile the slot can be filled to shed lustre on another human being. While the human beings are replaceable and expendable, the slots are nearly permanent.

In the beginning, the socialist states tried to prevent the emergence of a new ruling stratum of socialist bureaucrats. The principle behind this attempt was not so much one of overall social equality as the belief that no one should have too much in the conditions of poverty and disorder out of which socialism emerged. While the masses were suffering it would be immoral for the leaders to have too much. The material level of the skilled industrial worker was sufficient. Stalin put an end to this policy; at the same time he imposed additional severe privations on the population in order to build socialism in one country. Mao clung to his egalitarian ideas even though his own life style became quite luxurious. Egalitarian may be a bit too strong a term for Mao's ideas, which varied over time in response to changing circumstance. On the other hand, he was continually concerned that the benefits of the revolution were flowing disproportionately into the hands of bureaucrats and city dwellers while bypassing the mass of the population in the countryside. These inequities, he felt, were corrupting the revolution and posed a danger for the future. But his attempts to correct these defects failed before the Cultural Revolution and afterward.

Why did egalitarian–communitarian policies fail in China? Why for that matter have they failed just about everywhere?[3] Any competent Western sociologist would be likely to point out that revolutionary commitment is not enough to elicit substained effort over the long haul. For that purpose a series of material incentives graded according to the difficulty and importance of the task is necessary. This argument is probably correct. But is it a sufficient explanation? It is hard to see what bearing it has on the expensive way of life led by the top élite in China, Russia, and for that matter in the United States. People like that do not need all that money in order to be persuaded to do the work they are doing. They work, I suspect, for glamour, prestige, and in order to accomplish what they believe is worthwhile. Thus to explain the acquisition of super-comforts by the new dominant classes we may have to resort to a more general thesis. No matter what are the ideals with which they come to power, all élites facing a generally similar situation sooner or later behave in broadly similar ways. When they have the opportunity to take a disproportionate share of the goods that make civilization bearable, they take it. That has been true of the history of civilized societies in the East as well as in the West. In addition to the concept of differential incentives based on the division of labour we need some notion, such as a socially generated inclination to plunder, if we are to account for obvious facts. (Instead of plunder some social scientists might prefer a more neutral euphemism, such as over-appropriation of goods and services.) There is no need to attribute such an inclination to human beings in general. We are not talking about instincts here. Instead I want to draw attention to a process of social selection that both chooses certain types of personality for positions of leadership and then intensifies these personal traits by creating temptations, diminishing penalties for disapproved acts, and providing even greater rewards for the kind of behaviour that led to leadership in the first place. To be sure, where there are a large number of people discontented with their present leaders, one can achieve great esteem by behaving in a most unleaderlike fashion. St Francis of Assisi did exactly that. But the Franciscan movement broke apart shortly after his death precisely over the issue of property-holding by members of the order. The drive and ruthlessness necessary for an individual to rise toward the top of any social pyramid—or even to stay there—very likely has an aggressive component. As a Renaissance pope supposedly said, 'God gave us the papacy. Now let us enjoy it.' In a less candid form, such an attitude can surface anywhere.

In contemporary societies the candour disappears almost completely beneath a meritocratic mask, such as reward for services to the revolution, to humanity, or sometimes even for hard work. The distinction between plunder and performance of valuable services is not always easy to draw in specific cases. Yet one hardly needs to be an iconoclast to recognize that the distinction exists.

2 *Failures of both liberal capitalism and socialism*

By this time it is necessary to face directly the questions that underlie so much of social inquiry from the time of Socrates down to our own: What may be the implications of the evidence discussed here for the prospects of a free and rational social order in the foreseeable future? What are the obstacles and what forces favour such a development? The answers to such questions need not take the form of predictions and in my judgement should not. Rather they should describe and analyse a setting in which various actions are possible, including no action at all, the fate of most professional scholars. Like Max Weber, I believe that passionate political engagement is incompatible with the spirit of detachment and impartiality that serious scholarship requires. Nevertheless, scholarship can and does have significant political consequences when it shows the feasibility of various strategies and their probable costs in terms of an explicit set of values.

One stipulation is required at the beginning. We have to assume that nuclear destruction will not end life on this planet. This is an assumption about which many of us feel less confident than we did only a few years ago. However, without this assumption no effort to create a less miserable social order can make any sense.

As a starting-point we may take the prevailing widespread disenchantment with *both* liberalism and socialism as they have worked out in practice. This is a new historical situation. Previously there has been some part of the world to which people who wanted to change human society could point as a desirable model for the future. Revolutionary France and liberal England have served as didactic examples. So have fifth-century Athens and a largely imaginary Confucian China. The USA, Russia, and China are the most recent in a long historical development. Now that the big models have been discredited, the result, especially among many young people in the West, has been a turn toward hedonism or, more recently, religious fundamentalism, often with a generalized suspicion of all forms of secular authority. In my judgement such reactions do not promise viable political alternatives. Except in very simple and isolated non-literate societies anarchism is not a viable social arrangement. Some sort of central authority is necessary in more complex societies in order to co-

ordinate human activities, compose quarrels, and see to the defence
against enemies. Today most neo-anarchist social criticism, even with
the addition of Marxist colouring matter, impresses me as essentially a
form of self-indulgence. Such criticism depends parasitically on the
tolerance exercised by the objects of its criticism, mainly varieties of
liberal capitalism.

Yet the moral and intellectual rejection of both liberal capitalism and
socialism runs wider and deeper as an intellectual current than the
neo-anarchist critique. This larger current of rejection, as I perceive it,
emphasises three structural defects in liberal capitalism and a different
trio under socialism.

The main charge against capitalism stresses unemployment, the
terrible waste and human misery that results from the boom and bust
of the business cycle. Inflation has in recent years complicated and
even intensified fears of joblessness. The second failure of capitalism
has been the creation of what morally sensitive observers regard as
excessive inequalities of wealth and income. There is also overproduc-
tion in some areas, along with shortages and starvation in others. A
third defect is imperialism, or attempts to control and exploit weaker
states by a variety of means, in some cases including military force. For
reasons advanced elsewhere in print,[4] I do not believe we have any
good explanation of imperialism, at least not for the United States,
where the standard economic explanations just do not work. (Furthermore, such exploitation existed long before modern capitalism.) But
for the issues at hand, the absence of a satisfactory explanation is not
all that important. Imperialism exists, which is all we need to know.
The revolutionary and nationalist opponents of imperialism are there
too. Yet it is an abdication of human reason to assume that they will
necessarily be less repressive than the regimes they overthrow.

Presently existing forms of socialism emerged from revolutionary
victory in economically backward countries. So far it has been a
socialism of scarcity and oppression rather than of freedom and plenty.
Every inhabitant has to live in a bureaucratic straight-jacket tailored by
planners, propagandists, and the secret police. When, as in China during the Great Leap Forward, political leaders get carried away by their
own enthusiastic capacity for self-deception, the result is not greater
freedom and plenty. Instead it is exhaustion, chaos, and widespread
starvation. The bureaucracy becomes a monster that turns out to be
indispensable. Like the corpse in one of Ionesco's plays, long after its
proclaimed demise, it continues to grow and grow until its feet stick

out the door. There is nothing to be done except shrug the shoulders
and mutter about an incurable sickness of the dead. So socialists have
complained about bureaucratic deformation as the incurable malady of
socialism.

Another of the major stigmata of socialism as it actually exists is the
absence of intellectual freedom. This would be a bit more bearable
were it not for the suffocating presence of prescribed Truth on every
conceivable subject of human concern, from relations between the
sexes to how to grow rice. It is often said that the absence of intellectual freedom troubles no one except intellectuals, who are only a very
small segment of the population anyway. But where there is repression
of the intellectuals, the rest of the population is also the victim of
arbitrary oppression. No one is immune to the sound of booted police
clumping up the stairway in the darkness of the night to take off a loved
one to an unknown destination. Nor is it much better to face helplessly
the insults and threats of a raging crowd stirred up by one's enemies,
official or unofficial. To be sure this kind of violence has of late sharply
diminished in both the Soviet Union and China. But it has declined
mainly because high level officials do not want to be victims any more.
By no means has the suppression of dissidence disappeared. There is
very little in the way of institutional barriers to arbitrary terror, and
almost no barrier in doctrine or the more general cultural and moral
climate.

Finally, the system of inequality under prevailing forms of socialism
has turned out to be not very different from that under liberal capitalism. At the apex of the system there is a tiny élite whose official
position gives them access to most of the material goods of this life:
luxurious housing, fine food, chauffeured automobiles, in some cases
an airplane for private use, special access to health care and vacation
resorts, etc., etc. All that seems to be missing are fancy yachts. Smaller
motor cruisers do ply the Volga. Many belong to successful writers and
artists.

Looking now at the bottom of the social pyramid we find large
numbers of people who are forced to make do at the margin of
subsistence. In between these two extremes there are numerous grada-
tions from the official able to lead a quite comfortable life down to the
peasant who can make ends meet by dint of extra hard work. Thus the
range of inequality is essentially the same under socialism and liberal
capitalism. The main principle or justification—to each according to
his work—is the same in both societies, with roughly the same amount

of deviation from the principle in the practice of both societies. There is a difference in that judgements about the value of any specific kind of work have a much stronger political component under socialism than under liberal capitalism. It is also likely that there are many more people clinging to the rungs of the income ladder in the United States than in the USSR or China. Yet, to repeat, the number of rungs in the ladder and the differences in life styles between high and low rungs are very similar in all three of the societies discussed here.

3 *What cannot be done?*

Turning our attention to prospects for the future I will begin by taking a cue from a famous article by Lenin and ask: 'What *cannot* be done?' The most obvious answer suggested by the evidence discussed earlier is that one cannot eliminate bureaucracy. In a socialist society there has to be a bureaucracy to replace the allocation of goods and services through the market. To the extent that a capitalist society wishes to use criteria other than the market, as in the allocation of welfare benefits, or in the obtaining of goods and services, such as military hardware, that do not have a ready market price, a capitalist state also has to resort to bureaucracy. Finally, both socialist and capitalist societies have to make use of hierarchical controls in order to supervise the flow of raw materials and the application of human labour through the process of production. More briefly, a factory too has to have a bureaucracy.

The need for bureaucracy can be enough by itself to undermine and destroy egalitarian hopes, where such hopes exist. (I know of no evidence to show that they have ever been a mass phenomenon.) Other forces also work against egalitarianism. A fair amount of evidence indicates that for people to work hard there has to be a close connection between putting out the effort and getting the reward. One trouble with Chinese collective agriculture, a difficulty the new regime has tried to remedy, was that egalitarian arrangements broke the link between effort and reward. A peasant who worked hard on the collective farm might raise the total productivity and income of the farm. But since this increment had to be shared with all the others, the individual peasant would get for his pains no more than a tiny invisible fraction of his contribution to the collective welfare. On his own private plot, on the other hand, the connection between work and results was perfectly plain and quite satisfying. In that situation it made no sense to work too hard on collective property. Most peasants, in the areas from which this evidence comes, simply soldiered on the collective job for a few hours each day. The local cadres could do nothing about the situation.[5]

On these and other grounds, it seems plain enough that one cannot eliminate authority and social inequality from modern social arrangements. An influential tradition that goes back to Marx sees scarcity and the compulsion to work as the main source of repressive authority and unjustified inequality. A reduction in scarcity, both the 'artificial' kind of induced scarcity among the rich and the 'real' kind among the poor, might very well reduce the need for authority. Such a reduction in scarcity is, in terms of reducing human misery, something very well worth having in its own right, though on a world-wide scale the prospects now look very dim. But it is important to recognize that scarcity is not the only source of authority and inequality in human societies, perhaps not even the most important one. There is the need for discipline and social co-ordination mentioned from time to time in these lectures. There is the need for more rules and more ways to enforce them that arise from increasing numbers and increased crowding. Increased crowding is also likely to generate more quarreling and more need for ways to settle and prevent quarrels. Then there is the occupational structure of modern societies that is hardly likely to lead to anything approaching full equality of reward and esteem. Finally, in the absence of world peace there will always be the imperatives of military organization, certainly a decisive source of authority and inequality in contemporary societies.

If authority, especially bureaucratic authority, and inequality are likely to be prominent features of the social landscape for the foreseeable future, that does not mean there is absolutely nothing one can do. It merely means, as already suggested, that the egalitarian thrust is unlikely to accomplish anything. But there remains the huge, if perhaps more feasible, task of ensuring that social inequalities are rewards for scarce and socially desirable forms of competence. The airplane pilot who can land his plane repeatedly and safely under difficult conditions is a good example. So is the architect who can design a building that is inexpensive to construct and comfortable to work and live in. The obverse of the requirement of competence to justify authority would be a set of social mechanisms to prevent the privileged from appropriating their perquisites for purely personal ends.

To identify the socially necessary forms of special competence, to reward them in ways that elicit the best performance, and at the same time to prevent the misappropriation of scarce resources by an élite, constitute a set of very difficult tasks. Together they can provide the ingredients for sharp disputes. Every privileged class in human history has managed to create a rationale for its privileges in terms of its allegedly indispensable contributions to human welfare. To distinguish justifiable claims from self-serving rationalizations in such claims is no easy task. Yet one need not exaggerate the difficulties. In modern societies at any rate there is no great difficulty in spotting wealthy social parasites. Such persons do not even pretend to work. Instead they flit from one pleasure dome to another, according to fashion and the seasons.

Although controlling arbitrary authority and unjustified inequality is extremely difficult, under certain conditions it may not be altogether impossible. A parliamentary system with competing parties, based on a well-informed and relatively homogenous electorate is probably compatible with economic planning. Planning, along with measures for welfare, does diminish the sufferings of the poor, sufferings hard to justify in a wealthy society. Under such a system the planning apparatus would consist mainly of technicians, carrying out policies mandated by a parliamentary majority. To this extent there would be popular controls over the bureaucracy. It would be possible to extend these controls if there were a popular demand for so doing. On this score, however, there are grounds for skepticism. By and large, people are reluctant to do anything about the evils of everyday life, not to mention the more remote ones of government. They would rather grumble.

4 *Some preconditions of modern freedom*

For a relatively free form of socialism or socially controlled capitalism to emerge, in the first place the economy would have to have reached a high level of development. To maintain the system some sectors have to remain sufficiently profitable to support the social and welfare costs generated elsewhere in the economy. A central feature of such a society would be a two-sector economy. In one sector the government would control prices. Presumably this sector would turn out goods and services that were felt to have overriding social importance or could not yield a profit. In the other sector prices would be freely negotiated between sellers and buyers. Food products and goods that can be manufactured in small shops requiring little capital are among probable candidates. Planning would exist. State, social, and co-operative property would replace large-scale private ownership of the means of production.[6] Surely there would be conflicts between the two sectors and perhaps even more within each sector? Sharp rivalries and conflicts exist in all complex societies. The more important question is whether some group can gain overwhelming power through conflict or peaceful means and use its power to pursue asocial policies for its own benefit and to the damage of nearly everybody else. As such, socialism does not furnish the slightest guarantee that this will not happen. Neither for that matter, does liberal capitalism. The emergence of powerful groups happens all the time. We are told that an alert and well-informed electorate is the only real bulwark against anti-social policies by those in power. Perhaps that is true. On the other hand, an alert and well-informed electorate is among the rarest of species.

In the Scandinavian countries and Switzerland, export sectors have carried much of the load for paying for social services. Hence the economies of these countries, and others, have remained vulnerable to trends and decisions outside their borders. Every country, large and small, capitalist, socialist, or in between, is to a degree subject to the sanction of international markets. There is probably no way to eliminate this vulnerability.

A socialist or capitalist society with powerful democratic and liberal components could maintain itself, I suspect, only in a relatively safe back-eddy, one sheltered from the main currents and storms of international politics. Otherwise, nearly every domestic issue becomes entwined around the issue of the state's alignment in the international arena. Likewise, too many resources go into expensive military machines to permit extensive social programmes. On the other hand, if a state is able to remain aloof from the major international contests of the day, its leaders can from time to time enjoy the luxury of lecturing the Great Powers with moral advice that no one takes seriously.

To sum up, the prospects for a free and rational society seem to me bleak in the world's leading societies. Moderately free and rational societies may sustain themselves in marginal areas of prosperity, which are now confined to Western Europe. Even there, such societies appear to be examples of virtue parasitic on the vices of others, since they are heavily dependent on trade with the Great Powers. On the other hand, if one relaxes the conception of free and rational, other more encouraging trends appear. They deserve at least very brief comment because few observers, so far as I am aware, have called attention to them.

5 *Resurgence of parliamentary democracy*

Since the end of the Second World War there has been a resurgence
of parliamentary democracy that has reversed prior trends of the inter-
war era. The defeat of the Axis has led to the establishment of
democracies in Japan, Germany, and Italy. More recently, parliamentary systems have been set up in Portugal and Spain. After an interlude
of authoritarian government, Greece has returned to a parliamentary
regime. So has India, after a brief era of emergency rule. After a long
period of brutal authoritarian rule, Argentina has returned to democratic government, while Brazil too has been moving in that direction.
None of these regimes is altogether edifying, and in some instances
parliamentary democracy is still precarious. But from the standpoint of
justice and human freedom all of them are a great deal better than
their predecessors. There are then some objective reasons for hope
about the future of human institutions.

6 *Religious and chauvinist fundamentalism versus capitalism and socialism*

Over against these trends one must set the proliferation of religious
and chauvinist fundamentalisms all over the world. They seem to have
replaced the tarnished idols of liberalism and socialism. Prominent in
Iran and Lebanon, they are by no means invisible in Israel. Though in
India the Sikh movement has with good reason recently captured
world attention, the Mutiny of 1857, we should recall, displayed the
same religious fundamentalism, perhaps for the first time in modern
history as a serious political force. Northern Ireland presents the
spectacle of two fanatical groups locked in what looks like permanent
conflict. The United States displays similar trends sporadically but
thus far without the violence. Reactionary religious fundamentalism is
strong enough to be a factor that American political leaders must take
into account. Among Blacks in the US there have been a few episodes
of what was presented as black revolutionary violence. Evidently it
seems that an anti-rationalist virus has taken hold very widely in the
world though its virulence varies.

Perhaps more revealing is the widespread search for 'roots' in
American society. Adopted children want to know about their biologi-
cal parents, often to the distress of adoptive parents who have lavished
care and affection on their upbringing. Blacks want to know about
their African ancestors. Immigrant groups tout the virtues and values
of their country of origin. Patrician élites do the same about their
forebears, though an occasional iconoclast may express glee at raking

up a disreputable ancestor. Like the other movements mentioned here, the American search for roots reflects, I suggest, a current of opposition to a social order that judges people by performance and merit as measured by the market place, and a longing for a familiar world with secure social status and the traditional moral and intellectual certainties still intact.

This form of romantic nostalgia furnished much of the mass appeal of fascism over half a century ago. Fascism even displayed the same glorification of community that one finds in contemporary religious and chauvinist fundamentalism. Though these contemporary movements are not the same as fascism, there are enough similarities to make them ominous. Indeed, most of them are, upon inspection, ominous enough, without calling attention to their similarity to fascist movements, though the parallels help us to understand both. Where then do they come from? Discontent with modernization and its results is certainly a fundamental aspect of any explanation. By itself, on the other hand, it is inadequate. Two generations ago, by the time fascism was thoroughly defeated, most of these discontents would have fueled either Marxist movements or militant movements for reform within the liberal capitalist order. Now that both of these have lost much of their lustre, religious and chauvinist fundamentalist movements are taking their place by offering an image of the future and a cause to fight for. Fighting can be an excellent antidote for boredom and despair, especially for the young with limited prospects and tenuous social ties. Beirut and Belfast may be the images of the future rather than Orwell's bureaucratic nightmare. I certainly hope not. But I would like to have stronger grounds for hope than any I can presently discern.

There are, then, all around us, signs of social, cultural, and moral disintegration. They exist in both the capitalist and socialist camps. This situation has led a variety of observers to search the political skies for signs of a new synthesis or a new civilization to emerge out of contemporary neo-barbarism, just as Christian medieval Europe arose upon the fragments of antiquity. In addition to the fact that socialism has hardly turned out to be the new civilization some of these observers were looking for, there are good reasons for rejecting this superficially secular and curiously optimistic justification of the ways of God to man. There is no reason to expect social, cultural, and moral decay to be self-limiting or self-reversing. Death and collapse may be an equally likely outcome. For that matter decay is not the only process taking place, as we can see from the revival of liberal democratic governments.

In my judgement there is an even more important criticism to be made of this viewpoint. The element of despair in the diagnosis may often be on the mark or at least better than the platitudes of official liberalism and socialism. The remedy, on the other hand, is misleading and, often enough, dangerous. The call for, or claim to perceive, a new social and cultural synthesis is utopian. For reasons spelled out at some length in the preceding chapters, oppressive inequalities and violence seem likely to afflict humanity for a very long time to come. Mistaken promises about the end of evil lead to destructive disappointment, more violence, and more pain. Even worse, these supposed remedies for the sorrows and disasters of our time often amount to calls for the messiah or a transfusion of political glamour into a supposedly moribund body politic. Again, as I have tried to show in the preceding chapters, political glamour can be a disaster that produces enormous amounts of suffering. In some circumstances, to be sure, political glamour may be the only ingredient that will get desirable results, i.e. a reduction in human suffering. But the twentieth-century record shows that it generally intensifies suffering, and by no means only for the short run. The most severe cruelties of glamorous rulers have occurred only after they have supposedly secured their power. If humanity is to work its way out of its current plight—and I am far from sure that it can—there will have to be leaders at all levels who can turn their backs on political glamour and work hard for (barely) feasible goals rather than glamorous ones. All this is quite unexciting and in fact totally uninspiring. For that very reason it may be exactly what we need.

NOTES

Chapter 2

1. It is the great merit of Theda Skocpol, *States and Social Revolutions: A Comparative Analysis of France, Russia, and China* (Cambridge, England, 1979) to have given proper emphasis to this aspect.
2. Cora Dubois, 'The Dominant Value Profile of American Culture' in Paul Hollander (ed.) *American and Soviet Society* (Englewood Cliffs, 1969), 26.
3. For a review of the evidence see Seymour Martin Lipset and William Schneider, 'The Decline of Confidence in American Institutions', *Political Science Quarterly*, vol. 98, no. 3 (Fall, 1983), 379–402.
4. Lester C. Thurow, 'The Dishonest Economy', *New York Review of Books*, *XXXII*, no. 18 (21 November 1985), 34–5.
5. For a most imaginative study by a social psychologist of variations in attitudes toward authority see Stanley Milgram, *Obedience to Authority: An Experimental View* (New York, 1974). Critics who express outrage at this book seem to me upset by its surprising yet convincing findings about how cruelly human beings will behave in response to authority—as if all history did not teach a similar lesson! The most interesting aspect of Milgram's book is the material he gives showing the ways resistance to oppressive authority can arise. I have tried to present and reinterpret this material in my *Injustice: The Social Bases of Obedience and Revolt* (White Plains, 1978), 94–100.
6. Pauline Maier, *From Resistance to Revolution: Colonial Radicals and the Development of American Opposition to Britain, 1765–1776*, (New York, 1972) provides a good account of the changes in opinion that culminated in revolution.
7. *The Federalist*, No. 9 by Alexander Hamilton. See also No. 10 on the same theme by James Madison, where he gives an analysis of property and interest groups that resembles Marx.
8. Alfred D. Chandler, Jr., *The Visible Hand: The Managerial Revolution in American Business* (Cambridge, Mass., 1977) 87–88, 288–9.
9. For a different interpretation see William E. Nelson, *The Roots of American Bureaucracy 1830–1900* (Cambridge, Mass., 1982) esp. 5, 158–9. The author sees tension between the idea of majority self-rule and concern for protecting individual and minority rights as the main elements in the

history of governmental bureaucracy. The genteel reformers of the last half of the nineteenth century, known as the mugwumps, produced civil service reform, independent regulatory commissions, as the judiciary moved toward a more formal and abstract form of reasoning. It seems to me that this interpretation puts too much emphasis on high-minded reformers and not enough on structural changes in American society.

10. An early study of informal organization and still one of the best is Peter M. Blau, *The Dynamics of Bureaucracy: A Study of Interpersonal Relationships in Two Government Agencies* (Rev. edn., Chicago, 1963). I have also drawn on my experience of the bottom ranks of the bureaucracy in Washington during the Second World war.

11. Arnold S. Tannenbaum *et al.*, *Hierarchy in Organizations: An International Comparison* (San Francisco, 1974), 29–32, 120.

12. *Work in America*, Report of a Special Task Force to the Secretary of Health, Education, and Welfare (Cambridge, Mass., 1973), 13.

13. The Second Continental Congress deleted from the Declaration Jefferson's clause accusing the king of violating the rights of distant people and carrying them into slavery. But Jefferson's own position was highly ambiguous, to say the least. See David Brion Davis, *The Problem of Slavery in the Age of Revolution* 1770–1823 (Ithaca, 1975), 24, 169–84.

14. For a very good historical treatment of this theme see J. R. Pole, *The Pursuit of Equality in American History* (Berkeley, 1978). On contemporary aspects the study by Sidney Verba and Garry R. Orren, *Equality in America: Elite Values in Politics and Economics* (Harvard University Press, 1985), is most illuminating. The authors point out on several occasions that leaders of American opinion favour equality of opportunity but have very little sympathy for equality of results. The general public joins the leaders in opposition to the redistribution of wealth or equalizing incomes. The result, of course, is that unequal economic power spills over into unequal political power and influence. In a society formally committed to democracy and 'one person—one vote' this outcome can be somewhat disturbing. Yet the acceptance of economic inequality as supposedly the result of the race for life helps to legitimate political inequalities.

15. Nathan Miller, *The Founding Finaglers*, (New York, 1976), 77. From this somewhat journalistic but very useful account it appears that corruption has been rife in American history from the beginning down to the present day.

16. James Bryce, *The American Commonwealth* (2nd rev. edn., Toronto, 1891), II, 616.

17. US Bureau of the Census, *Statistical Abstract of the United States 1985* (Washington, DC, 1984), table 717, p. 433.

18. Stanley Lebergott, *The American Economy: Income Wealth and Want* (Princeton, 1976), 6–9.

19. Lebergott, *American Economy*, 6–9.

20. *Statistical Abstract of the United States 1985*, table 759, p. 455.

21. *Statistical Abstract of the United States 1985*, table on 'Weighted Average Poverty Levels Based on Money Income . . . : 1970–1983', p. 429. According to the *New York Times*, 4 November 1983, p. D16, David A. Stockman, then director of the Office of Management and Budget, asserted that the number of poor people in the United States was less than two-thirds of the total officially reported by the Bureau of the Census. The official poverty count, he pointed out, is based only on money income and ignores the 107 billion dollars in kind, medical, housing, food, and other aid that raises the living standard of many low-income families.

22. *Statistical Abstract of the United States 1985*, table 734, p. 442.

23. *Statistical Abstract of the United States 1982–83*, table 648, p. 386.

24. On the culture of this rapidly growing professional and technical sector see Joseph Bensman and Arthur J. Vidich, *The New American Society: The Revolution of the Middle Class* (Chicago, 1971), esp. Part III.

25. *New York Times*, 11 December 1983, p. 28.

26. Lester C. Thurow, 'The Disappearance of the Middle Class', *New York Times*, Sunday, 5 February 1984, p. F5.

27. *Statistical Abstract of the US 1985*, tables 774, 775, p. 463 on shares of wealth; table 758, p. 454 on poverty level.

28. Lebergott, *The American Economy*, 161–75, esp. 174–5. But his conclusion that the percentage of total wealth concentrated in the top group has not changed is at variance with the figures cited above from the *Statistical Abstract of the US 1985*.

29. Christopher Jencks *et al.*, *Inequality: A Reassessment of the Effect of Family and Schooling in America* (Harper and Row, New York, 1973), 226. First published by Basic Books, New York, in 1972.

30. Christopher Jencks *et al.*, *Who Gets Ahead: The Determinants of Economic Success In America* (New York, 1979), 217.

31. Jencks *et al.*, *Who Gets Ahead*, 226, 294.

32. Jencks *et al.*, *Inequality*, 227.

Chapter 3

1. Marc Bloch, *La Société féodale* (Paris, 1949), II, 350–1.

2. Fritz Kern, *Gottesgnadentum und Widerstandsrecht im früheren Mittelalter: Zur Entwickelungsgeschichte der Monarchie* (Leipzig, 1914).

3. For a study of such movements between 1762 and 1907 see Victor Leontovitsch, *Geschichte des Liberalismus in Russland* (Frankfurt am Main, 1957); also George Fischer, *Russian Liberalism* (Cambridge, Mass., 1958).

4. *Grundzüge der Geschichte Russlands* (Stuttgart, 1949), 28–9.

5. Hoetzsch, *Grundzüge*, 56–7.

6. P. Miliukov, *Ocherki po istorii russkoi kul'tury* (4th edn., St Petersburg, 1900), I, 192–202. For a fuller treatment of political trends see the 1909 (6th) edn. of this work, I, 137–252.

7. For details see Thomas C. Owen, *Capitalism and Politics in Russia: A social history of the Moscow merchants, 1855–1905*, (Cambridge University Press, 1981).

8. Barrington Moore, Jr. *Soviet Politics: The Dilemma of Power: The Role of Ideas in Social Change* (Cambridge, Mass., 1950), 30–1.

9. Moore, *Soviet Politics*, 32.

10. For sources and more detail on the early history of democratic centralism see Moore, *Soviet Politics*, 64–71.

11. Moore, *Soviet Politics*, 145–6.

12. Leonard Schapiro, *The Origin of the Communist Autocracy: Political Opposition in the Soviet State; First Phase 1917–1922* (London, 1955), 188–9.

13. Moore, *Soviet Politics*, 150–1.

14. Schapiro, *Communist Autocracy*, Chap. III, esp. pp. 48–51.

15. Quoted in Moore, *Soviet Politics*, 128.

16. Schapiro, *Communist Autocracy*, 261. A later Soviet author discussing this period speaks of the 'compression' of local soviet democracy at this time and the rise of decision-making by individuals instead of broad collectives. See Moore, *Soviet Politics*, 129 and source cited.

17. The first new elections occurred in 1926. For the Party view of the results and what they were supposed to accomplish see the decree of the Central Committee of 20 July 1926, in *KPSS o rabote sovetov: sbornik dokumentov* (Moscow, 1959), 211–22, esp. 219–20.

18. *KPSS o rabote sovetov*, 298–302. For some additional details see Moore, *Soviet Politics*, 136–7.

19. *KPSS o rabote sovetov*, 472–82.

20. Moore, *Soviet Politics*, 159–60.

21. V. I. Lenin, *Sochineniya* (4th edn., Moscow, 1950), vol. 27, 241. The quotation occurs in the article on labour discipline in the *Bol'shaya Sovetskaya Entsiklopediya* (2nd edn., Moscow, 1952), vol. 14, 487. A very similar quotation from the same speech—Lenin had no objections to repetition for the sake of emphasis—occurs in the article on one-man management, *BSE*, vol. 15, 476. All references citing the *BSE* are from the 2nd edn., 1949–58.

22. Moore, *Soviet Politics*, 164–5. Quotation from Lenin, *Selected Works* (New York, n.d.), VIII, 92.

23. *BSE*, s.v., 'Yedinonachaliye', vol. 15, 475.

24. *BSE*, s.v., 'Yedinonachaliye', vol. 15, 475.

25. Barrington Moore, Jr., *Terror and Progress—USSR* (Cambridge, Mass., 1954), 63–7.

26. *BSE*, s.v., 'Sotsialism', vol. 40, 153, and 'Distsiplina trudovaya', vol. 14, 486–7.
27. Quoted in Moore, *Soviet Politics*, 176.
28. Moore, *Soviet Politics*, 178, citing Leon Trotsky, *Sochineniya* (Moscow and Leningrad, 1927), vol XV, 180, 181, 198, 201.
29. Moore, *Soviet Politics*, 181.
30. Alec Nove, *An Economic History of the U.S.S.R.* (London, 1969), 94.
31. Nove, *Economic History*, 104.
32. Nove, *Economic History*, 139–42.
33. Nove, *Economic History*, 106.
34. Nove, *Economic History*, 106, 122.
35. For an excellent review of how the Bolsheviks saw their problems see Alexander Erlich, *The Soviet Industrialization Debate* (Cambridge, Mass., 1960).
36. Nove, *Economic History*, 150–1, 153.
37. Nove, *Economic History*, 157, 166.
38. Quoted in Nove, *Economic History*, 165.
39. The figure comes from Nove, *Economic History*, 167.
40. Nove, *Economic History*, 179–80.
41. James R. Millar, 'Mass Collectivization and the Contribution of Soviet Agriculture to the First Five-Year Plan: A Review Article', *Slavic Review*, vol. 33, no. 4 (December, 1974), 750–66. See esp. 751, 754, 759, 760.
42. Millar, 'Mass Collectivization', table 3, p. 762.
43. Nove, *Economic History*, 180; on Stalin, 178.
44. Millar, 'Mass Collectivization', 763 citing Jerzy F. Karcz, 'From Stalin to Brezhnev: Soviet Agricultural Policy in Historical Perspective' in James R. Millar (ed.,) *The Soviet Rural Community* (Urbana, 1971), 42.
45. Nove, *Economic History*, 191.
46. Nove, *Economic History*, 207. See also 205–6.
47. Nove, *Economic History*, 190–1, 202.
48. Joseph Stalin, *Problems of Leninism* (Moscow, 1941), 371–4.
49. Nove, *Economic History*, 209.
50. Robert Conquest, *The Great Terror: Stalin's Purge of the Thirties* (London, 1968), 543.
51. An acute reader for the Oxford University Press remarked at this point that Marx resembled German professors of the period whereas Lenin's polemics were a cross between those of the journalist and the guttersnipe. To me it seems that Marx in his more abusive moments, especially in his treatment of Bakunin and Lassalle, also became a full-blown guttersnipe. These are not trivial matters. A good social and cultural history of polemical styles would reveal a great deal about politics.
52. Conquest, *Great Terror*, 38.
53. Conquest, *Great Terror*, 6–7.
54. Conquest, *Great Terror*, 27–30, 36–8.

55. Moore, *Terror and Progress*, 177.
56. Conquest, *Great Terror*, 36.
57. See Conquest, *Great Terror*, 538–9 for a list of Politburo members; Chap. 2 on Kirov's murder.
58. Conquest, *Great Terror*, 484–5.
59. *BSE*, vol. 50, 424.
60. Moore, *Terror and Progress*, 155.
61. Alex Inkeles put this argument most forcefully. See the long quotation in Alexander Dallin and George W. Breslauer, *Political Terror in Communist Systems* (Stanford, 1970), 105–6.
62. Conquest, *Great Terror*, 491.
63. Moore, *Terror and Progress*, 155.
64. Conquest, *Great Terror*, 516, based on unofficial claims.
65. Marshall I. Goldman, *USSR in Crisis: The Failure of an Economic System* (New York, 1983).
66. Seweryn Bialer, *Stalin's Successors: Leadership, stability, and change in the Soviet Union* (Cambridge, England, 1980), 156.
67. Mervyn Matthews, *Class and Society in Soviet Russia* (New York, 1972), 143.
68. Bialer, *Stalin's Successors*, 95; see also 45–6.
69. Bialer, *Stalin's Successors*, 168–9.
70. Bialer, *Stalin's Successors*, 169–77.
71. Murray Yanowitch, *Social and Economic Inequality in the Soviet Union: Six Studies* (White Plains, 1977), 114, 88.
72. Yanowitch, *Social and Economic Inequality*, 80.
73. Walter D. Connor, *Socialism, Politics, and Equality: Hierarchy and Change in Eastern Europe and the USSR* (New York, 1979), 200–7. See also Matthews, *Class and Society*, 298; Yanowitch, *Inequality*, 131.
74. Bialer, *Stalin's Successors*, 188.
75. Yanowitch, *Inequality*, 38–9.
76. Yanowitch, *Inequality*, 39–40.
77. Executive pay from *Business Week*, 9 May 1983, pp. 84–5. According to the *Statistical Abstract*, 1982, table 664, p. 400, the average annual total compensation for all domestic industries in 1981 was only $20,372. Both mining and communications, however, ran over $30,000. Average includes managerial salaries and workers' wages.
78. Yanowitch, *Inequality*, 30.
79. Yanowitch, *Inequality*, 32.
80. Matthews, *Class and Society*, 113.
81. Yanowitch, *Inequality*, 39, table 2.6.
82. Leonard Joel Kirsch, *Soviet Wages: Changes in Structure and Administration since 1956* (Cambridge, Mass., 1972), Chaps. 4, 5.
83. Matthews, *Inequality*, 88–9.
84. Yanowitch, *Inequality*, 141–6, 151.

85. Yanowitch, *Inequality*, 39.
86. Connor, *Socialism, Politics, and Equality*, 231; for occupational prestige ratings see ibid., 93 and Yanowitch, *Inequality*, 104–5.
87. Connor, *Socialism, Politics, and Equality*, 235.
88. Connor, *Socialism, Politics, and Equality*, 81, 263–6.
89. Yanowitch, *Inequality*, 52–3.
90. Bialer, *Stalin's Successors*, 156.

Chapter 4

1. G. William Skinner, editor, *The City in Late Imperial China* (Stanford, 1977), 233–4. See also the map of Chinese cities in the form of end-papers. Further citations to articles by the editor will take the form of Skinner, *City*; other contributors will be identified.
2. Skinner, *City*, 23–4.
3. Skinner, *City*, 268. The cultural and social role of the merchants and artisans, however, deserves much fuller investigation. It is intriguing to come across brief statements by other Sinologists describing trends in China during the principal urban surge between the eighth and the eleventh centuries AD, which have close parallels with the rise of urban civilization in Europe from about the thirteenth century onward. They include relative peace and order, commercial transformation, technical innovation, and philosophical speculation. By Chinese standards the country in the eleventh century reached its highest point in terms of 'political stability and free discussion'. See E. A. Kracke, Jr., 'The Chinese and the Art of Government', in Raymond Dawson (ed.), *The Legacy of China* (Oxford, 1964), 313–14. Another author speaks of a 'striking increase in the number of independent and creative minds and an unprecedented expression of individual tastes in art and culture' under the Sung. See Wm. Theodore de Bary, 'Individualism and Humanitarianism in Late Ming Thought', in Wm. Theodore de Bary and the Conference on Ming Thought, *Self and Society in Ming Thought* (New York, 1970), 148; see also 8. In the Chinese context, on the other hand, these trends did not, so far as I have been able to discover, form part of any drive by the city dwellers for political objectives.
4. Sybille van der Sprenkel, 'Urban Social Control', in Skinner, *City*, 609.
5. Skinner, *City*, 336.
6. L. S. Vasil'ev, *Agrarnye Otnosheniya i Obshchina v Drevnem Kitae* (Moscow, 1961), 210–11.
7. Tso Chuan, Duke Hsiang 31 (542 BC), as translated in Burton Watson, *Early Chinese Literature* (New York, 1962), 63.
8. Brian E. McKnight, *Village and Bureaucracy in Southern Sung China* (Chicago, 1971), 5, 83, 142–7, 181–5.
9. Richard J. Smith, *China's Cultural Heritage: The Ch'ing Dynasty, 1644–1912* (Boulder, Colo., 1983), 45.

10. Smith, *China's Cultural Heritage*, 120.
11. For a valuable case study see Howard J. Wechsler, *Mirror to the Son of Heaven: Wei Cheng at the Court of T'ang Tai-tsung* (New Haven, 1974).
12. Laurence A. Schneider, *A Madman of Ch'u: The Chinese Myth of Loyalty and Dissent* (Berkeley, 1980) provides a valuable history of this set of ideas.
13. Smith, *China's Cultural Heritage*, 42.
14. Max Beloff, *Soviet Policy in the Far East 1944–1951* (London, 1953), 55.
15. Richard C. Thornton, *China: A Political History, 1917–1980* (Boulder, Colo., 1982), 231, 234.
16. Frederick C. Teiwes, *Politics and Purges in China: Rectification and the Decline of Party Norms 1950–1965* (White Plains, 1979), 199, 271.
17. Thornton, *China*, 240–1.
18. James R. Townsend, *Political Participation in Communist China* (3rd impr.; Berkeley, 1969), 105.
19. This impression is based in large measure on the detailed history of Chinese politics to be found in Teiwes, *Politics and Purges*.
20. Richard Curt Kraus, *Class Conflict in Chinese Socialism* (New York, 1981), 5.
21. C. K. Yang, 'Some Characteristics of Chinese Bureaucratic Behavior', in David S. Nivison and Arthur F. Wright (eds.), *Confucianism in Action* (Stanford, 1959), 145.
22. Teiwes, *Politics and Purges*, 238.
23. Teiwes, *Politics and Purges*, 631.
24. Assar Lindbeck, *The Political Economy of the New Left: An Outsider's View* (New York, 1971), 32–3.
25. Steven W. Mosher, *Broken Earth: The Rural Chinese* (New York, 1983), 276.
26. Bao Ruowang (Jean Pasqualini) and Rudolph Chelminski, *Prisoner of Mao* (New York, 1973), Chaps. 1–4.
27. Martin King Whyte, *Small Groups and Political Rituals in China* (Berkeley, 1974), 231.
28. Whyte, *Small Groups*, 233.
29. Teiwes, *Politics and Purges*, 115, 121.
30. Cf. Mosher, *Broken Earth*, 78–9.
31. Teiwes, *Politics and Purges*, 513, 603.
32. Mosher, *Broken Earth*, 58.
33. Mosher, *Broken Earth*, 62–4.
34. *China Aktuell*, July 1985, summary #50, p. 428, citing *Xinhua News Agency* (Beijing), 10 July 1985, according to BBC, *Summary of World Broadcasts*, Part III, 16 July 1985; *Radio Guangzhou*, 8 July 1985, according to BBC, *Summary of World Broadcasts*, Part III, 12 July 1985. *China Aktuell* is a German press and radio monitoring service. It is especially valuable for its coverage of the provincial press and radio in China.
35. Quoted in Teiwes, *Politics and Purges*, 536.

36. Teiwes, *Politics and Purges*, 539, see also 543.
37. Teiwes, *Politics and Purges*, 514. The quotation appears to be taken from a statement by Mao made in May 1962, but one cannot be certain of the year since Teiwes does not give that information.
38. For Mao's account of his own change of heart see Bonnie S. McDougall, *Mao Zedong's 'Talks at the Yan'an Conference on Literature and Art'*, A trans. of the 1943 Text with Commentary, Michigan Papers in Chinese Studies 39 (Ann Arbor, 1980), 61.
39. Teiwes, *Politics and Purges*, 245.
40. Teiwes, *Politics and Purges*, 337.
41. Kraus, *Class Conflict*, 151.
42. Townsend, *Political Participation*, 57 gives the text of this part of the resolution.
43. James Pinckney Harrison, *The Long March to Power: A History of the Chinese Communist Party, 1921–1972* (New York, 1972), 346.
44. Harrison, *Long March*, 65.
45. Harrison, *Long March*, 204–9; quotation from 206.
46. Jürgen Domes, *The Internal Politics of China 1949–1972* (New York, 1973), 114–15.
47. Nicholas R. Lardy, *Agriculture in China's Modern Economic Development* (New York, 1983), 151.
48. Thomas P. Bernstein, 'Stalinism, Famine, and Chinese Peasants: Grain Procurements during the Great Leap Forward', Pamphlet, East Asian Institute, Columbia University (Elsevier Scientific Publishing Company, Amsterdam, 1984), 370.
49. Bernstein, 'Stalinism, Famine, and Chinese Peasants', 350, 365.
50. Roderick MacFarquhar, *The Origins of the Cultural Revolution: The Great Leap Forward 1958–1960*, vol. 2 (New York, 1983), 28 with reference to sources.
51. MacFarquhar, *Origins*, II, Chap. 2.
52. For a brief official description that gives the flavor of the Stalinist period see *Kratkaya Sovetskaya Entsiklopediya* (Moscow, 1943), 1279–80, s.v. 'samokritika'.
53. By no means do all rectification campaigns involve public criticism of cadres. The first large-scale rectification campaign occurred in 1940, according to Harrison, *Long March*, 271. There was another big one in Yanan in 1942. For some revealing documents see Conrad Brandt, Benjamin Schwartz, and John K. Fairbank, *A Documentary History of Chinese Communism* (Cambridge, Mass., 1952), 372–419. Public criticism of local cadres did take place before the Communist victory of 1949. William Hinton, *Fanshen: A Documentary of Revolution in a Chinese village* (New York, 1966) describes the events in Long Bow during the spring and summer of 1948 in fascinating detail. Thus all the main features of rectification—originally a Confucian concept—were in place by the time

the Chinese Communists took power. For a good brief exposition of their place in the new regime see Teiwes, *Politics and Purges*, Chap. 1.

54. Teiwes, *Politics and Purges*, 532. Good account in Anita Chan *et al.*, *Chen Village: The Recent History of a Peasant Community in Mao's China* (Berkeley, 1984), Chap. 2.

55. A. Doak Barnett, with a contribution by Ezra Vogel, *Cadres, Bureaucracy, and Political Power in Communist China* (New York, 1967), 171.

56. See also Teiwes, *Politics and Purges*, 549–50, for further mention of suicides.

57. Barnett, *Cadres*, 169.

58. Teiwes, *Politics and Purges*, 546–53, esp. 549.

59. Kraus, *Class Conflict*, 148–9.

60. Teiwes, *Politics and Purges*, 549.

61. Teiwes, *Politics and Purges*, 62 provides a good summary of what is known. For more detail see Harrison, *Long March*, 212–17.

62. Teiwes, *Politics and Purges*, 630–1.

63. Stuart R. Schram, '"Economics in Command?": Ideology and Policy Since the Third Plenum, 1978–84', *China Quarterly*, no. 99 (September, 1984), 437–49. Schram's whole article, 417–61, is a perceptive review of the doctrinal discussions accompanying what I have called the course toward meritocracy.

64. Lardy, *Agriculture*, 89.

65. Chan *et al.*, *Chen Village*, 268–9 for date; Lardy, *Agriculture*, 217 for spread of system.

66. Chan *et al.*, *Chen Village*, 268–9, 274.

67. *China Aktuell*, September 1984, summary #40. p. 500, citing *Xinhua News Agency* (London), 9 September 1984.

68. *China Aktuell*, September 1985, summary #41, pp. 602–3, citing *Renmin Ribao* (Beijing), 17 August 1985, as reported in BBC, *Summary of World Broadcasts*, Part III (Reading), 31 August 1985. The *Summary* in this case devotes three columns to this *Renmin Ribao* report.

69. Lardy, *Agriculture*, 217.

70. Chan *et al.*, *Chen Village*, 270–1.

71. Martin King Whyte and William L. Parish, *Urban Life in Contemporary China* (Chicago, 1984), 33.

72. Whyte and Parish, *Urban Life*, 53.

73. Whyte and Parish, *Urban Life*, 64–8, 71.

74. Whyte and Parish, *Urban Life*, 73.

75. Whyte and Parish, *Urban Life*, 55.

76. Whyte and Parish, *Urban Life*, 56.

77. On changes in industrial management see also Schram, ' "Economics in Command?": Ideology and Policy Since the Third Plenum', 454–6.

78. *China Aktuell*, October 1984, pp. 579–83 gives an excellent commentary by Erhard Louven on the Chinese Party's Central Decision of 20 October

1984 on industrial reform. The text of the decision is on pp. 584–99. My comments stem from Louven's commentary and pp. 587–8 of the text.

79. Whyte and Parish, *Urban Life*, 103.
80. Whyte and Parish, *Urban Life*, 62–3, 272–3. Some evidence, however, has come to light indicating that university education can be a passport to good jobs. In the more than 5,800 large and medium sized state-controlled plants 74 per cent of the cadres have a university education. Among factory directors 89 per cent have such an education. Party secretaries have 81 per cent. This situation is new and is said to represent a sharp increase over the recent past. But what proportion of university graduates manage to land these jobs is not indicated in the reports summarized in *China Aktuell*. See the issue of September 1985, summary #37, p. 600, citing *Jingji Ribao*, 6 September 1985, according to BBC, *Summary of World Broadcasts*, Part III, 14 September 1985, and *Xinhua News Agency* (Beijing), 12 September 1985, according to BBC, *Summary of World Broadcasting*, Part III, 14 September 1985.
81. *New York Times*, 2 June 1985.
82. Whyte and Parish, *Urban Life*, 42; see also 40–1, 55 for some reasons for the drop.

Chapter 5

1. I have simplified a complex course of development here. For a very perceptive and fuller treatment see Albert O. Hirschman, *The Passions and the Interests: Political Arguments for Capitalism before Its Triumph* (Princeton, 1977).
2. For an excellent brief survey with emphasis on the USSR see Alec Nove, *The Economics of Feasible Socialism* (London, 1983).
3. See Rosabeth Moss Kanter, *Commitment and Community: Communes and Utopias in Sociological Perspective* (Cambridge, Mass., 1972). The Israeli kibbutz is a limited exception in so far as the link between variations in work and income has been severed, with all members receiving roughly equal access to material goods. Variations are supposed to be according to need. But there are frequent complaints about members being unwilling to do their share of disagreeable jobs. Different degrees of authority also exist despite the theoretical supremacy of the members' assembly. The best single account, because it gives the historical background and places the kibbutz in the context of Israeli society, is Paula Rayman, *The Kibbutz Community and Nation Building* (Princeton, 1981).
4. Barrington Moore, Jr., *Reflections on the Causes of Human Misery and Upon Certain Proposals to Remove Them* (Boston, 1972), 116–32.
5. Mosher, *Broken Earth*, 39–43; Anita Chan *et al.*, *Chen Village: The Recent History of a Peasant Community in Mao's China* (Berkeley, 1984), 173–4.
6. Alec Nove, *The Economics of Feasible Socialism* (London, 1983), 211, 227.

INDEX

agriculture: Soviet early land reform 49–50; Soviet collectivization 51–2, 54, 89–90; range of incomes in USSR 67–8; capitalist reforms in Chinese 96–8; *see also* New Economic Policy

authority *see* bureaucracy, inequality, law

Bao Ruo-Wang (Jean Pasqualini) 82
Barsov, A. A. 52
Beloff, Max 75–6
Beriya, L. P. 59
Bernstein, Thomas P. 90
blacks, American: 30, 31
Bloch, Marc 37
Bolsheviks: early democratic ideas 38, 39; on inequality and terror, 7–8; *see also* Lenin, Stalin, Terror
Breznev, L. I. 6
Bryce, James 29
bureaucracy: and market 6, 7, 80–1; necessary in modern economy 21, 22, 80, 119; five managerial hierarchies compared 24; differences under capitalism and socialism 26; and pre-industrial meritocracies 27–8; corruption in Soviet 55; imperial and Chinese compared 69–71; Soviet and Chinese Communist compared 78–9; Chinese Party controls over 81–2, 86–7; corruption in Chinese 83, 84–7; as socialist avenue to success 113–14; *see also* egalitarianism, inequality

Campaign against Spiritual Pollution in China 95–6
capitalism and socialism: historical origins of 104–6; in Marxist–Leninist theory 9, 38–9, 43, 106; similarities in 109; some structural defects of 117; limits of social criticism under 110–11
capitalism, liberal: and inequality in USA 26–7, 33–4; shared traits in West 108–9
'capitalist roader' 110
Catholic Church 27–8
Censorate, Imperial Chinese 74
Cheng, village of 72
Cistercians 27
collectivization of agriculture (USSR) 52–3, 54, 89–90
collegiality 44, 45
Communist Party, Chinese: mass support for 75, 91–2; bureaucratic structure of 76–8; and small-group controls 81–3; factional infighting in 83; and egalitarian-cooperative ethic 95, 107; theory and practice compared with Soviet 107–8; *see also* Bolsheviks
Connor, Walter D. 67
Conquest, Robert 56, 62
corruption: and tax evasion in USA 28–9; forms of and controls over in Chinese bureaucracy 83, 84–7; in Soviet bureaucracy 55
Cultural Revolution: and large group control 83, 91–2, 93, 94; *see also* small-group controls

Declaration of Independence (USA) 28, 29
democracy: resurgence of 123, 125; elements in pre-modern Russia and China, 37, 72–3; in early Bolshevik beliefs 38, 39; and Soviet 'proletarian' 47–8
democratic centralism (USSR) 39
Deng Xiaoping: capitalist reforms in agriculture 12, 96–8, 100, 108
De Tocqueville, Alexis 4
doctors' plot, Soviet 61

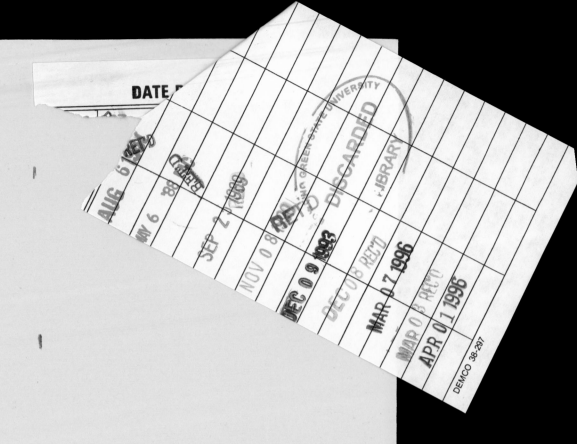